Sunday's Fools

Every game has its winners and losers and the ordinary sports story touts the top dog. But Tom Beer's career in the NFL has been downhill all the way and his wry perspective from the bottom of the heap underscores this unique view of the game of professional football.

After an outstanding career as a college player for the University of Houston, Beer was selected for several All-American football teams and for the College All-Star Game in Chicago against the Green Bay Packers. He then played for the Denver Broncos and the New England Patriots — teams that lost steadily and consistently during his years with them. Beer retired from an active career in the game with a knee injury and has spent the time since reflecting on the follies and foibles of a sport that engrosses millions of fans and grosses millions of dollars each season.

Written with a light touch and a strong sense of the absurd, the story is nevertheless not always a funny one. Beer takes a relentless look at the recruitment of collegiate players, the game as seen through the eyes of the ignorant rookie, the pressure on coaches and players, the off-field activities of the players, and the connivings of the press for the "hot"

continued on back flap

continued from front flap
story. His account of the effects of extended losses on an entire pro organization from head coach to water boy is both harrowing and hilarious.

Finally, Beer reflects on what happens to players who never do make it to the top, muses on the changes in the game, and ponders the hope held out to the game of professional football by the new World Football League for which he now works.

Sunday's Fools

Stomped, Tromped, Kicked, and Chewed in the NFL

by TOM BEER with George Kimball

Illustrated with Photographs

HOUGHTON MIFFLIN COMPANY BOSTON

1974

First Printing c

Library of Congress Cataloging in Publication Data

Beer, Tom.
  Sunday's fools.

  1. Beer, Tom. 2. National Football League. 3. Football.
I. Kimball, George, joint author. II. Title.
GV939.B43A37   796.33'2'0924 [B]   74–12417
ISBN 0–395–19952–2

Printed in the United States of America

1812109

For my parents. You stood by me
in my darkest hours. Thanks
for the guiding light.

And for Marilyn.

Preface

My PURPOSE IN WRITING this book isn't to exploit any person, place, or thing I've come in contact with over the past six or seven years of my professional football career. On the contrary.

The Bernie Parrishes and the Dave Meggesys and the Gary Shaws have all made their points, many of them well taken, but I don't really have that ax to grind. While I've certainly experienced my share of heartbreak and disappointment I don't really regret it. My old Denver coach and current Buffalo Bill head man Lou Saban used to call us worms. Well, I managed to spend an entire career encased in a can of worms. It wasn't fun, but I can look back on the experience without rancor now that it's over.

Many books have been written about great football teams, great football coaches, great football players. Vince Lombardi and Tom Landry and Hank Stram and Don Shula and Len Dawson, Jim Kiick and Larry Csonka have all graced the shelves of many a bookstore.

But what those 100,000,000 or so beer-bellied, foul-mouthed

football fanatics — don't get me wrong; I love them — sometimes fail to realize is that for every winner there are a lot more losers.

And what about losing? Many astute coaches have described the difference between winning and losing as a fine line, yet the fan rarely glimpses life below that fine line.

The guys who went out and busted their asses every Sunday during the fall — busted their asses only to go down to defeat — are rarely heard from outside the pages of their hometown papers. And even then the discussion is usually a clichéd treatise on how "We're gonna do better next week."

Try being a laughingstock sometime! Do you think the Denver Broncos and New England Patriots of this world *like* getting the crap kicked out of themselves every week? Nonetheless, I firmly believe that God placed some of us on this earth to be losers, because there sure are a lot more losers than winners. If everyone won, what fun would a game be, right?

This is the story of the Harold Stassens of the National Football League.

Contents

Illustrations

Sunday's Fools

1

In the Beginning

THE PHONE RANG that warm spring afternoon in my room at
Baldwin House, the dormitory accommodating the University of Houston's varsity athletes. It was March 8, 1967, a
day I'd been especially looking forward to. It was the day
that comes once a year — the day of the professional football draft, when the destiny of some 442 college seniors is
determined.

With the NFL-AFL merger the preceding year, the days
of astronomical contract figures and bidding wars were
gone. I was a year too late. Much of the mystery and
confusion was also eliminated. Gone, too, were the "baby
sitters," the businessmen employed by the NFL to watch
over top players. My sitter had been Bob Nussbaum, a successful Dallas businessman. Before he had said his farewells, though, he had introduced me to a lovely Houston girl
who loved football players. I had decided Nussbaum was an
all-right guy in my book.

On the other end of the line was Ted Nance, the sports information director for the University of Houston. "I just got

a call from Denver," he said. "If you're available in the second round the Broncos are going to select you."

"Oh, shit!" was my initial reaction. "Who the hell wants to play with Denver?"

I was a cocky, starry-eyed All-American, and I saw myself taking over Marv Fleming's job at Green Bay, or perhaps Jim Gibbons' in Detroit. I'd been described by pro scouts as one of the premier tight ends in the '67 college crop, and in my hasty evaluation of tight ends around the league I'd already confidently determined that I was better than most of them.

"*Denver?* Why Denver," I kept thinking. I'm a star. I'd received a personal telegram from Vince Lombardi telling me how much the Packers wanted me. The Dallas Cowboys had been corresponding with me for over two years. They'd even written my parents a letter explaining the advantages of playing in "Big D."

The Denver Broncos had not, I knew, had a winning season since their inception. I could remember watching AFL games on television when I was a kid back in Detroit. The only thing I could recall about the Broncos was that they used to wear hideous, vertical-striped stockings and had the ugliest uniforms I'd ever seen.

I'd even seen them play the past year at Rice Stadium against the Houston Oilers. The Oilers had won 45 to 6, while the Broncos had something like fifteen yards total offense and perhaps two first downs. (Some of the veteran Denver players would later recall watching the films of that game: "We had a half a reel of offense, a half a reel of defense, and four kicking reels.") Denver had played a game devoid of hustle or enthusiasm.

My dreams of grandeur with some established, winning team were already starting to evaporate at the mere *idea* of being drafted by Denver. And with the merger I'd have no choice but to go. I could already see myself stepping in a pile of fresh road apples on a Denver back street.

At approximately 1:15 P.M., Central Standard Time, I received a call from the Broncos. A strange voice on the other end said in dramatic tones, "Welcome to Denver, climate capital of the world." "Gee, thanks," I thought. "I do have a touch of asthma." On the phone in Denver was Fred Gehrke, the director of player personnel. It suddenly dawned on me that being drafted in the second round meant big money, lots of it. Fred assured me that we would have no problem coming to terms.

*

He couldn't have been more wrong. As soon as Gehrke met with my financial adviser, Frank Skyzmanske, and me a month later in Detroit it was clear that we were miles apart. The initial demands and offers on both sides were pretty comical. I wanted $200,000 for three years, plus a new car, a motorboat and trailer, and clothes. The Broncos countered with a package of $50,000 spread over three years. In layman's terms, they were offering me $15,000 a year plus a $5000 bonus for signing. It occurred to me that everything I'd heard about the Broncos since I'd been drafted was true. They were cheaper than Jack Benny. We shook hands with Gehrke and he left.

Skyzmanske was very cheering. After Gehrke had walked out the door, in his heavy Polish accent he muttered, "*Screw him!"* There's nothing like that kind of assurance in time of need.

The next several months were spent worrying. I didn't hear another word from the Broncos, and while I talked with several Canadian teams, their offers were as paltry as Denver's. I finally devised a scheme to prod the Broncos into action.

A friend of mine worked for the school paper, the *Daily Cougar.* I told him that I was considering an offer to sign with Montreal of the Canadian Football League for $100,000. Hell, I didn't even know the Montreal team's nickname, but from the *Cougar* the item was picked up by the Houston dailies. Shortly thereafter I heard from the Broncos. Thanks again, Frank.

I signed on June 3, 1967, for $92,500, which, all things considered, wasn't too bad for the son of a Detroit cop. I was now a full-fledged, bucking Bronco.

The next weekend I flew to Denver to formally sign my contract and meet with Lou Saban, the Broncos' new head coach. After a successful AFL coaching career with Buffalo, Saban had left to rejoin the collegiate ranks as head coach at the University of Maryland after the 1965 season. The Broncos had lured him back to the pros with a ten-year contract as head coach and general manager.

Needless to say I made a complete fool of myself in Denver. I spouted off like a sperm whale in heat. Clichés like "We're going to win this year" and "I can help this club" rolled off my tongue faster than you could say colorful Colorado. I was all Joe College, a real hot dog for the Denver media. I'm surprised some of my new teammates didn't come over to my motel, break down the door, and beat the hell out of me once they'd read the papers.

But I fell in love with Denver immediately. It's a beautiful city. The scenery is breathtaking, with the Rocky Mountains rising up to the sky only a few miles away. The people are great, and the best-looking girls in the whole world seem to flock to the mile-high city.

The Broncos organization, on the other hand, was a frightful mess. Lou Saban had taken over the sickest of franchises. The stadium was antiquated, and even the team offices were in cramped quarters atop the Lucas Building in Adams County.

Before the season Saban had practice facilities erected on a plot of land due north of the offices. Some of the veterans complained; as dilapidated as it was, they'd have preferred to practice at Bears Stadium.

I later discovered that free beer was given away after each practice by the Coors distributorship directly across the street from the stadium.

I noticed bumper stickers all over town reading "Go with the New Broncos." I felt proud to be a "New Bronco," along with the number one selection, Floyd Little of Syracuse. Our rookie crop also included Notre Dame's Pete Duranko and George Goeddeke and a giant from Ohio State, Mike Current.

The balance of the roster, though, was hardly filled with household names. Jason Franci, Marvin "Butch" Davis, Lee Bernet, Max Wettstein, and company were all rather forgettable football players who had lasted as long as they had by virtue of the fact that they toiled for the Broncos. Our quarterbacks were Max Choboian, Scotty Glacken, Jim "King" Corcoran, and Mailon Kent.

On Sunday morning at a golf course about forty-five minutes from Denver, I was apprehensive about meeting my new coach, but not nearly as terrified as I'd learn to be. We chatted for half an hour or so over ham and eggs. He hardly ever smiled. Right away I started to worry. "He's pissed off because I held out for so long," I was thinking, "or maybe at something I said in the papers."

I learned later that the only time Saban smiles is after winning football games.

2

Chicago

I MADE MY FIRST MISTAKE as a pro on August 4, 1967. I played in the farcical College All-Star game at Soldier Field in Chicago. It's supposed to be quite an honor, but in retrospect I'd say its most singular effect — besides the ever-present chance of injury — is that you're losing the time you might have put in practicing with the professional team that signed you. I'd estimate that playing in the All-Star game set me back as much as two thirds of a season.

With five, the Broncos had the most players of any team assigned to the All-Star roster. But no matter how much the game might've hindered us, it was fun. Most of the guys on the team that year were good drinkers, and we spent most of our time in Chicago having a good time. Just imagine all that money housed under the same roof! Onassis would have flinched. Mel Farr was there with his canary yellow Jaguar, but I was disappointed in Gene Trosch. Kansas City's number one choice was only driving a Riviera.

The coaches, by and large, were great guys. Their only problem was that they had difficulty teaching the fundamentals of football. Head coach Johnny Sauer was in his last year with the All-Stars. He's a good sportscaster but an unsuccessful coach. The previous year his squad had lost to the Packers by a score of 39 to 0. We improved on that, but not by much; the Pack rolled over us 27 to 0.

*

We received our game-plan package on the Sunday prior to the Friday night game. I suppose Sauer was using some sort of reverse psychology, but I know that I heard so much about the has-beens and old men that made up the Pack that I was actually overconfident. I found myself thinking, "I hope we don't beat them too badly. I wouldn't want to see any of those old guys get hurt."

Sauer compared Elijah Pitts, the great running back of the Packers, to our Nick Eddy. To hear him tell it the two were exactly alike, except for a couple of factors: Pitts was stronger and faster.

As Sauer rambled on in his evaluation of the Packers, Rod Sherman, a talented flanker from USC, was cracking up. An enraged Sauer began to scream at him, "If you don't like it here, Sherman, you can go back to Southern Cal!" Sherman called Sauer an idiot and then chuckled along with the rest of the squad.

Rod sat on the bench for the entire game and watched us get creamed by the "old men."

It was true that we were younger, bigger, and no doubt faster than the Packers. What Johnny Sauer didn't mention was that they had two small advantages working for them — experience and a guy named Vince Lombardi.

We were completely outcoached.

Sauer's method for selecting certain starters is worth mentioning. After practicing twice a day for four weeks, the decision of which players would start the game was left to chance. Sauer flipped a coin. If that wasn't bad enough, it was a strictly "Heads I win, tails you lose" proposition.

After flipping the coin to choose the starters, the winners were announced to the 90,000-plus spectators. The player would run through a maze of cheerleaders while some collegiate band played a few bars of his school song. It was sort of an All-Star tradition. The hitch was that the players who were announced didn't start and the ones who started weren't announced. You figure it out.

To add insult to injury, the band played "The Eyes of Texas," the University of Texas fight song, when I ran through the cheerleader gauntlet. The bastards didn't even know the Houston song.

Our flight back to Denver was scheduled to depart O'Hare Airport at eight the next morning. I wouldn't be coached by Johnny Sauer anymore, I thought to myself. I slept well.

3

The Rookies

WE WERE AWAKENED at six the following morning and driven by limousine to the airport. I was tired and beat up. Dave Robinson, a Packer linebacker, had done a number on my jaw and lower lip with his tree-trunk forearm. Once the plane was in the air, the stewardess came around with some Irish coffee. After the fourth cup my aching body became slightly numb.

The Dallas Cowboys entourage was also on the plane in the company of their director of player personnel, Gil Brandt. They were on their way to the Cowboys training site at Thousand Oaks, California. I felt I knew Brandt personally even though we'd never been formally introduced. He must've sent me a dozen letters and various Cowboy propaganda releases when I was in college. I disliked him instantly. He said the Cowboys were going to draft me. The Dallas organization was one of the best in the National Football League. And here I was going to one of the worst.

He came over and shook hands with us, congratulating us on the game the past night, and wished everyone the best of luck. All of a sudden he didn't seem like such a bad guy any longer. I felt like asking him to do something, to rescue me from going to Denver. I was already homesick for Texas. I also knew Dallas needed a tight end.

*

The two-hour plane ride gave me the chance to discuss the Broncos' practice schedule and camp regimen with tackle Mike Current. Current had spent some time in the Denver camp prior to being summoned to Chicago to replace an injured All-Star, Ron Billingsley. Players always worry about the rigidity of practices. We don't like to be worked hard, and it seems as though we're always finding coaches who thrive on being slave drivers.

After we arrived at the Denver airport amid the popping of flash bulbs and the whirring of television cameras, we were transported by Fred Gehrke to the Bronco training camp at the Holiday Inn, a mile from the practice field. The coaches were waiting for us in the coffee shop. Most of the players were resting in their rooms; the team had an exhibition game scheduled for that night against the Detroit Lions.

Coach Saban welcomed us and said little else. It occurred to me that all the pomp and glitter of being an All-Star was over and done with. No more interviews, picture-taking, and general pampering from the gentlemen of the press. I was just a struggling rookie trying to make the team. My stomach felt like a pretzel. I was starting all over again.

I could sense that the Bronco players were nervous on the bus to the stadium. This was, after all, Denver's big chance at the big time, the first meeting between an old, established NFL team and a fledgling club from "the other league."

The pregame betting line must have been in the 45-to-0 point range. The Lions players no doubt came to Denver anticipating a cakewalk. They were, after all, the co-favorites (with the Packers) to win the infamous "Black and Blue" Central Division of the NFL and featured stars like Wayne Walker, Earl Morrall, Ron Kramer, Gail Cogdill, and Pat Studstill.

Before the game I shook hands with the Lions' head coach, Joe Schmidt. He had been one of my idols when he'd played in Detroit in the years I was growing up there. I'd wanted to play in Detroit so much I could still almost taste it. Besides the fact that it was home, the whole organization had class. Their uniforms even sparkled — Hawaiian blue and silver, with a lion decal on the helmet.

By contrast, the Denver uniforms were ugly, antiquated, orange and blue rags that reeked of mothballs and invariably had been patched at least a few times. At least, though, Saban had banished the helmet decals of previous Bronco years. It had been a goofy-looking creature that was exactly like the horse Lee Marvin rode in *Cat Ballou.*

*

The five All-Star game participants were introduced to the 25,000 fans just before the game. Goeddeke, Current, Duranko, Beer, and Little. I supposed the Broncos were trying to give the fans something to cheer about before the imminent debacle. I was excited as I ran through the goal posts to our bench. So what if I was in street clothes? Somehow the roar of a partisan crowd does something to an athlete, and the Denver fans were great that night. Both Floyd Little and myself received tremendous ovations; I guess the Denver fans thought we were the two saviors come to bail out the pathetic Bronco offense. They were half right. Floyd is one of the finest running backs in the National Football League to this day.

That night, August 5, 1967, history was made. For the first time ever an AFL team defeated an established NFL club when the Broncos won 13 to 7. I was happy for my new teammates. Some of them like Bob Scarpitto and Charlie Mitchell had labored unrewarded for many years wearing the Bronco colors. There seemed to be a promise now of respectability, a chance to be a winner. For the first time I felt proud to be part of the Denver organization.

I couldn't fully share in the postgame merriment because I hadn't played, but I was proud of the way our guys stuck in and scrapped for the entire sixty minutes.

Perennial All-Pro defensive tackle Alex Karras of the Lions had boasted that if the Broncos beat Detroit that night he would personally walk back to the Motor City. He got a head start. Apparently his frustrations brimmed over to the breaking point, and midway through the third period Alex got into a fight with one of the Broncos and was thrown out of the game. He walked off the field to the ecstatic roar of the victory-crazed hometown crowd. This was the biggest thing to happen in the Rockies since the discovery of gold, people were saying. Lou Saban could have run for mayor of Denver the next morning and walked away with the election without uttering a sentence.

"This," shouted Saban, "is the biggest victory in Bronco history!" The players were equally ebullient. "We beat a helluva good team without our five star rookies," said one veteran to a reporter. "Just wait'll they're ready. We're on our way. Move over, Kansas City. Here comes Denver!"

The players savored the victory on Sunday, consuming plenty of Coors at a local pub. My new teammates were hoping the day would never come to an end. Their fantasies, however, came to an abrupt halt on Monday morning as Saban started working us for the next exhibition game.

The veteran players were understandably pissed off when the coach extended the two-a-day workouts in order to allow the All-Stars to catch up on lost practice time. I found myself the object of the evil eye from some fatigued veterans on a number of occasions, and it seemed as if I kept hearing the word "bastards" slip from various tongues whenever one of us All-Stars happened to be in the vicinity.

The first practice in Denver was one I'll never forget as long as I live. It was pure, agonizing hell, a nightmare. I'd speculated, but I'd never really known, how difficult it would be to practice in that sort of altitude before. I knew now. I couldn't breathe.

Saban had us running all the time, from one drill to the next, from one coach to another. We'd run the ropes, hit the two-man sled, hit the seven-man sled, run, run, run. After half an hour of drills I was exhausted, and all I had to look forward to was the toughest part of practice. Pass patterns and running plays, timing and execution.

I wanted to lie down under a tackling dummy and die. I couldn't catch my breath or even think. Everything seemed

dark and distant. My throat was parched and my nasal pas-
sages were clogged in the low humidity, and my lungs felt
seared as I tried to gasp for oxygen.

Another factor adding to my pain was our quarterback situation. We had Choboian and Glacken and Corcoran and
none of them could throw a football with much accuracy,
meaning that with my ass dragging I still had to chase all
over the damn field in pursuit of errant passes. Clearly, we
were going to win no championships with any of them calling signals.

Saban was aware of this, of course, but he overreached
himself. On August 15 he made his biggest blunder since
he'd traded "Mad Bomber" Daryle Lamonica from Buffalo to
Oakland. Lou surrendered the Broncos number one draft
choices for 1968 and 1969 for an untested, little-used
back-up quarterback from San Diego, Steve Tensi.

Tensi had been John Hadl's understudy with the Chargers
and had rarely played. Saban's move was a gamble, and it
was a gamble that ultimately would spell doom for his
coaching reign in Denver. You cannot win in professional
football without the leadership of a talented quarterback.

Tensi, it would develop, was not that leader — but by the
time Saban found that out, the two number one picks were
long gone.

•

Tensi joined the club in workouts just before our August 18
meeting with the Minnesota Vikings. He looked more like a
country and western singer than a pro football player. He
wore his hair in a flattop with high, swept-back ducktails

along the side, circa 1958. He also wore white moccasins, had those Joe Namath–like stooped shoulders, and he idolized Elvis Presley.

But the moment he stepped out on the field with a football, he was a player. He didn't have an arm, he had a bazooka, and he had a knack for making the difficult pass route easy for the receiver. All you had to do was run under the shot, look up, and catch it. It would be there.

Tensi had only been in camp a few days, though, and in the game against the Minnesota Vikings Saban started Choboian — out of respect more than anything else. Choboian was known for reasons devoid of irony as "Maxie the Taxi," and when he failed to generate any offense the crowd of 30,000, chomping at the bit, began a chant of "We want Tensi!" throughout the first half.

The game was still roughly even when Tensi entered the game midway through the third period. The fans cheered madly, and the big guy responded by marching us down the field. He threw several beautiful passes to Eric Crabtree and Al Denson to set up our final touchdown, and we hung on to defeat the Vikings 14 to 9. We'd been the first AFL team to beat an NFL team, and now we were the first and only team to do it twice in a row. The city of Denver went stark, raving mad. We were now the Cinderella team of the AFL and fast on the rise. This time I personally felt part of the victory. I'd started the game and contributed my share. I celebrated with my teammates. Players were already making early predictions. "We can win it all with Steve," said one veteran. Several of the players echoed the statement that we could do it in '67.

Over the tumult in the locker room I heard Coach Saban shouting that it was the most important victory in the history of the Denver Broncos. I remembered he'd said the same thing after we'd beaten the Lions. I learned that he said that whenever we won a game.

◦

At practice Monday some of the guys were starting to horse around in their exuberance. They were in for a rude awakening; celebration time was over. Saban blew his stack. "You people better shape up and forget about the past," he raged. "Last week is history. Get your asses in gear or you'll be out on the Valley Highway tonight." The Valley Highway, Denver's main drag, was Saban's personal metaphor for hell. It actually ran from Cheyenne, Wyoming, to Raton, New Mexico. He had them fearing for their jobs, if not lives. Players started hitting again.

All week long he kept bringing in new bodies to "look at." It was his policy that anyone who might conceivably help the ball club was worth a tryout. Players, understandably, resented the policy. After all, there's not much security in professional football to begin with, and then when you've worked your tail off day in and day out to beat a guy out for a position, it's disheartening as hell to show up the next morning and find two new guys in his place.

So many bodies passed through Saban's turnstile that eventually the players said "to hell with it" and started to joke about the situation. Our captain, Dave Costa, would pull aside younger players and warn them, "Don't screw up or you'll be on the Valley Highway tonight." "Do your job, rookie, or hit the Valley Highway," Big Dave would snarl in jest. On one play in practice two rookie linemen jumped offside and a voice roared out from the defense: "You guys are in trouble! It's against the law to hitchhike in pairs on the Valley Highway!"

Saban loathed stupid mistakes, and when he spotted one he could reduce you to feeling two inches high with a fierce, silent stare. Offsides, backfield in motion, missed blocking assignments were but a few of the mental errors he truly detested.

Another thing that made it tough was the relentless Colorado sun combined with a lack of water. Saban didn't believe in water on the practice field. Sometimes an injured player who was jogging on the sidelines would fill his helmet with ice and smuggle it to the other players. You simply can't imagine how much pleasure can be derived out of sucking on an ice chip during an exhausting practice. At moments like that, if I'd been given a choice between Raquel Welch or Ursula Andress or sucking on an ice cube the ice would have won hands down.

❋

We played our final preseason game in the well-known community of North Platte, Nebraska, against the powerful Oakland Raiders. The game was staged there, allegedly, to commemorate the Nebraska State Centennial. North Platte's claim to fame is that it was the home of Buffalo Bill Cody. We flew into town on a Frontier airlines propeller-driven job. The flight was horrible. A few of the veterans could remember the last time the team had flown on a prop flight, back during an airline strike.

We landed between haystacks on the North Platte strip. It turned out that that's how the runway was marked. I never did find out how planes land there at night. I suppose they set a torch to the haystacks.

A police escort took us to the Holiday Inn. The Raiders were housed in some hole in "downtown" North Platte. My buddy Rod Sherman told me after the game that the hotel the Oakland team stayed in had been built by old Buffalo Bill himself. There were no televisions, the furniture was strictly turn-of-the-century, and the (single) beds had more humps than a camel.

*

That evening the city fathers had planned an evening commemorating the historic occasion. I'm sure they meant well, but the whole affair turned out to be nothing short of disastrous.

The Honorable Norbert T. Tiemann, governor of Nebraska, was the guest speaker at a banquet. He welcomed both clubs and then proceeded to extol the virtues of the great state of Nebraska. After his speech each player was introduced and presented with a certificate proclaiming him an "Honorary Citizen of Nebraska." Then the festivities began. We were ushered into another room to partake in "Las Vegas Night." Local yokels were dressed up like old-time gamblers and dealers, and there were tables for blackjack, roulette, and poker.

We were given a stack of Confederate money to use as a stake, and then at the end of the night, prizes were auctioned off. The players with the most Rebel capital could purchase gifts.

The auction began methodically, and eventually several players got fed up with the slow pace of the proceedings and began to crowd the prize table. Before anyone knew what was happening, they were grabbing prizes off the table, engaging in tugs of war over fishing reels and flashlights while the Confederate money flew around in the air. The night ended prematurely.

We went by bus to the local high school field the next morning for the game. A press box had had to be specially built to accommodate the television crews. Constructed of two-by-fours, the thing shook so badly when the wind blew that the cameramen were hanging on for dear life. The stadium itself seated around 3000, but there were about 10,000 spectators there to see us put our winning streak on the line against the Raiders. We had heard rumors that the Raiders were still going through two-a-days and were dog-ass tired. They played like they were, in any case, and we won 21 to 17.

After the game Coach Saban locked the door, said a prayer, and then, you guessed it, told us it was the most important victory in the history of the Broncos.

As the pilot taxied the plane down the runway, negotiating his way through the haystacks, I leaned back in my seat eagerly awaiting the start of the regular season. "Goodbye, North Platte!" I thought. "Bring on the Patriots."

4

The Long Season

NINETEEN SIXTY-SEVEN was going to be our year. The Year of the Horse. In just four short weeks Lou Saban had transformed the cellar-dwelling patsies into a powerhouse contender in the AFL's Western Division. At least that's what the Denver players and our diehard fans had been led to believe. Bears Stadium, as it was then known, was sold out for the league opener against the Boston Patriots. Thirty-five thousand four hundred fans had purchased tickets for the nationally televised game pitting Saban's youth movement against Mike Holovak's old vets.

It was my first encounter with Bears Stadium. The field had been designed, of course, for baseball, and it was only as an afterthought that football was ever played there at all. The lighting was so bad that we played our nighttime exhibition games at the University of Denver's field. The turf at Bears Stadium was high and clumpy, and each week huge chunks of sod would be ripped up over the course of a game. Dead center on the fifty-yard line a huge blue and orange Bronco helmet had been chalked onto the grass. Once the elements had taken their toll on this configuration, any player who had the misfortune to fall into it came up looking like a fugitive from a body-painting class.

At the south end of the stadium were the bleachers, occupied each week by the so-called "South Stand Super Fans," a group of several thousand vociferous maniacs who earned, over the years, the right to be called the worst in all of pro football. The South Stand Super Fans actually made the Kansas City "Wolfpack" sound like a schoolboy choir. One of their more endearing qualities was that they showed up every week prepared to heap as much abuse — frequently physical as well as verbal — on the Broncos as on the opposition.

In the years preceding my arrival, the South Stand Super Fans had usually provided most of the highlights at Bronco games, for as crude and obnoxious as they could be, they were usually more exciting than the Denver Broncos. In the course of one bygone season, just after the Kansas City Chiefs had demolished the Broncs by some forty points, the Super Fans had pelted Hank Stram's contingent incessantly as they left the field, using everything from beer and whiskey bottles to snowballs and rocks. The Chiefs had been forced to regroup and huddle en masse in the middle of the playing field while the police tried to disperse the football-crazed fanatics. The Super Fans weren't angry because the Chiefs were stomping the Broncos so badly — that happened all the time — but because Stram's scrubs, trying to show off their rarely displayed talents, had resorted to a couple of bombs late in the game. The South Standers, believing the Chiefs were trying to run the score up, took offense. They finally ran out of ammunition.

But they were equally capable of going to work on the hometown team. Once the Broncos had opted to sit on a tie against the Miami Dolphins and run out the clock to finish a 10-10 game. Queried about his strategy after the game, Saban told reporters that "half a loaf is better than none." The next time the Broncos played at home the South Stands were directing their uproar at the Denver bench from the first whistle, and as the Broncs proceeded to get buried, loaves of bread rained on the Denver bench throughout the fourth quarter.

By 1967 the city fathers of Denver, reasoning that if players were going to get hurt at Bears Stadium it should be by each other and not by the spectators, outlawed the sale of bottled beer inside the stadium. This did nothing to rectify our next biggest obstacle, the locker room facilities. Back in the days when Buffalo's War Memorial Stadium held a solid lock on first place for the poorest facilities in pro football, Denver was generally accepted as having the second worst. Buffalo had nosed us out largely on the fact that we, at least, had showers that worked. Otherwise the place resembled a cross between a medieval dungeon and a musty London air raid bunker. There was rarely any hot water, and even then it was only there for the first fortunate few who used the showers. It was, in short, a minor league facility hosting what was supposed to be major league football.

We practiced hard all week, looking forward to playing games for real, but the fact that we had a three-game winning streak swelled a few heads. People were playing grab-ass on the field, telling jokes when they should have been listening, and I could sense that as a whole our team's mental attitude was not what it might have been. We were cocky, and we were all confident that the Patriots would die in the mile-high altitude. Our twenty-two-year-old lungs would hold up better than their thirty-year-old ones would.

For the first time in years we'd been installed as three-and-a-half-point favorites. We suited up fourteen rookies for the game, making us the youngest team in professional football by a wide margin.

The weather that morning was made to order for the Rocky Mountain Chamber of Commerce, crisp, fresh air on a sunny Sunday afternoon. After battling the veteran Patriots evenly for the first half of the game, we started to slip, and they led 21-16 early in the fourth period. Then a Steve Tensi–to–Al Denson fifty-eight-yard bomb set up a field goal by Gary Kroner, and we'd closed it to 21-19. A minute or so later Goldie Sellers picked off one of Babe Parilli's passes and scampered in for the touchdown without anyone laying a hand on him, and we were ahead, 26-21, after the extra point. The game ended that way when Nemiah Wilson picked off another pass — our sixth interception of the after-noon — and we had hung on to win what Coach Saban called (yes, again) "the most important game in Bronco history."

As was his wont before and after each game, Saban exhorted us to "talk to the man upstairs." (In our present state of exhilaration we felt more or less on equal footing.) Almost immediately afterward the first wave of reporters hit the locker room like a swarm of bees and the place was alive with media people for over an hour. We were whooping it up in the showers, raising all sorts of hell, and when someone yelled across the room, *"One down and thirteen to go!"* someone else instantly retorted, *"Hell, one down and fifteen to go!"* referring, of course, to the AFL Championship and Super Bowl games.

*

The Oakland Raiders were next on the agenda, the same Oakland Raiders we'd beaten in North Platte, Nebraska, a month before. Easy pickings.

Brimming with confidence, we dogged it all week long during practice, and on Thursday, defensive day, Saban exploded. He ripped the entire squad for slipshod practices and lackadaisical attitudes. "You guys better buckle on your jocks," he shouted, "because the Raiders are going to knock them down your throats."

Lou had a way of icily staring from one individual to the next and driving a point home without much dialogue. If nothing else, he succeeded in scaring the shit out of us. Not just the rookies either. He told veteran tackle Bob Breitenstein that if he persisted in blowing blocking assignments he would not be wearing a Denver uniform much longer. We finished practice that day in a terrified silence. Saban could come on like some sort of supernatural villain from a Vincent Price movie. We weren't even thinking about the Raiders — we were totally spooked by the coach.

*

On Sunday, September 10, the Denver Broncos were pulled off cloud nine. I suppose that as rookies we had underestimated the problems inexperience can bring, and Oakland murdered us, 51-0. We played in a daze. Could this be the same Oakland team we'd beaten in North Platte?

The answer, of course, was that it was *not* the same team. The Raiders we'd played before were engaged in an exhibition game, trying out new personnel and various combinations as they experimented for the upcoming season when the games counted. This one had counted.

I felt totally humiliated and embarrassed. A high school team would have played a better game than we did. The Raiders dominated every phase of the game except punting. That's because we had to punt twelve times. They ground out 208 yards on the ground for four touchdowns, and their quarterbacks accounted for another 180 yards and two TDs in the air. Our offense contributed a minus fifty-three yards passing and minus five yards in total offense.

I thought the veins in Saban's temples were going to explode. He looked as if he wanted to decapitate each and every one of us with his bare hands. He flayed us after the game, tearing us apart individually and collectively. "Remember practice last week?" he bellowed. "If I *ever* see or hear of a Denver player goofing off in practice again he'll be out on the Valley Highway!" Enough said. He sounded as though he meant it.

The plane trip back to Denver was a flying morgue. Occasionally you'd hear cards being softly shuffled or a beer can being opened. Some players felt so chastised they felt guilty about drinking the beer. I hadn't known what it would be like to lose under Saban. Now I did, and believe me, I was frightened.

*

The team meeting Tuesday was like waiting for the executioner. The whole team was there nearly an hour early, waiting for the arrival of The Man. When he arrived I also discovered that Lou Saban was a man of his word. Bob Breitenstein, who had missed a few blocks on Sunday, was no longer a Bronco.

Larry Kaminski and George Goeddeke had coined the term "Pit City" for the Tuesday meetings. They had a running contest to see who would wind up with the sweatiest armpits after watching the game films. Naturally, the worse a player had performed in the game, the more he'd sweat from the ordeal of seeing his mistakes recapitulated in the presence of the coaches. When all is said and done, after all, a professional athlete does take this sort of thing seriously. It's his bread and butter; if he doesn't produce he doesn't play; if he doesn't play, he doesn't get paid.

With closed mouths and renewed hustle we began to prepare for our next foe, the expansion Miami Dolphins. The amalgamation of rookies and castoffs had finished dead last with a 3-11 record in 1966. The local papers, as eager as we were to forget the Oakland fiasco, dug up the fact that our quarterback Steve Tensi had a personal two-game winning streak over Miami; he'd beaten them with four touchdown passes the year before, and during the exhibition season while still with the Chargers, he'd thrown a last-minute pass to give San Diego a 20-19 win over the Dolphins.

We flew into Miami that weekend in the middle of Hurricane Beulah, and the winds buffeted the plane up and down for the last hour of our descent, throwing loose objects all over the cabin. I silently prayed that it wasn't an indication of things to come. Unfortunately, it was.

The Dolphins, scoring in every quarter, led 14 to 0 at half time, and while we came back briefly to tie the game in the fourth quarter, Abner Haynes, a former Bronco, scored twice — including a touchdown on a sixty-five-yard breakaway — to help beat us, 35-21. Tensi didn't throw any touchdown passes, thank you.

I nearly passed out from exhaustion after the game. Playing in Miami in the middle of September is like playing a July road game in hades.

⁂

Saban quietly told one Denver writer that we had to "bleed a little before we grew." We were bleeding. All the rah-rah talk of championships and winning records had diminished to a dead, very frightened silence. Everyone was fearing for his job. There was no security on a team like the '67 Broncos — nor is there, in fact, on any team that's going downhill fast. Players were being cut each week and new bodies brought in to take their places. Players like Roger Le-Clerc, a place kicker, and Rick Duncan, another kicker, were claimed on waivers from Chicago; Tom Cichowski, a much-needed offensive tackle, was obtained from the Green Bay Packers.

After the loss in Miami Saban made wholesale changes. With the arrival of LeClerc, our place kicker Gary Kroner, whose kick-offs had been leaving us in the hole, became expendable. That same week Saban also gave Scotty Glacken his walking papers. Glacken was a bonus baby from Duke who'd supposedly received $100,000 to sign. Big money, the veterans were joking, for a guy who couldn't play quarterback.

LeClerc was by then a veteran on the way down. He'd been Denver's number one draft pick in 1960 and Chicago's fifteenth. One day I asked him why in hell he hadn't signed with the Broncos since he stood to collect a lot more money as a first-round selection there.

"It's a funny thing," replied Roger. "I got a telegram from Denver telling me I was their number one selection, but I never heard anything else from them. I wasn't even sure it was legit."

With the addition of several more new players that week, we suited up nineteen rookies for the game against the New York Jets. It was obvious that, win or lose, Saban was going to go with youth and build for the future. A few more veterans would be pared from the roster as each week passed.

*

A capacity crowd filled Bears Stadium to see the Jets, and, naturally, to see Joe Namath. I confess to awe at just being on the same field with him for the first time, and no less imposing was the foundation of his pass protection, Sherman Plunkett. Big Sherm weighed around 350 pounds, although the program had him listed at a meager 310.

The game lasted thirty-nine minutes and eight seconds too long, and by the time it was over I was even more in awe of Joe Willie. We'd opened up looking like we were going to run the Jets right off the field, and by the second quarter we'd run up a seemingly commanding 24-7 lead.

Then Namath went to work. Masterfully beating the clock, he brought them back to 24-21 just as the half ended. In the second half he tore our defense apart for two more touchdowns and a field goal while our offense was completely smothered. We never scored another point. Namath ended up with twenty-two completions and 399 yards passing as we lost, 38-24. Broadway Joe was magnificent; he was worth every penny of that $400,000 the Jets had signed him for. The South Stand Super Fans stood in tribute and gave him a standing ovation after the game.

Several of us went out and drowned ourselves in Coors, already apprehensive about Tuesday's meeting with Saban. We were making bets on who would be cut that week, on how many new players would be brought in this time. Someone pointed out that we'd find out early that week. We were scheduled to assemble for the team picture at 10:00 A.M. on Monday.

※

Monday morning arrived, and players stood around in uniform on the practice field, quietly chatting in small groups. Everyone was there except the coaches. Thoughts immediately rushed to mind: they were plotting against us. They were crowded around the waiver wire, checking for bodies. Live bodies, dead bodies, it probably made little difference. They finally arrived. No one said a word. Saban kept staring, first at one guy, then at another. It was kind of humorous if you like sick humor. He'd start walking toward a group of players, and they'd disperse and start walking away. It was like herding frightened cattle. Then the coach would turn and walk toward another group and the first one would relax.

Not a word was spoken while the picture was being taken. We'd have to go through this paranoid anxiety again the next day. We rushed off to steel our nerves with more Coors.

On Tuesday morning we discovered that one of our co-captains, four-year veteran Gene Sykes, was no longer with us. He'd been our starting strong safety, and his assignment on Sunday had been trying to cover tight end Pete Lammons. Lammons had caught eight passes for 141 yards. Sykes's place was taken by rookie Jack Lentz, and we now had twenty first-year players on our forty-man roster.

When we took our 1-3 record to Houston to play the Oilers, the game was billed as the "Kiddie Bowl." Houston had fourteen rookies on their squad.

During pregame warm-ups I spotted a group of my old teammates from the University of Houston in the stands. I was swelling with pride at my opportunity to show off in front of the collegians. Here I was playing big-time pro football!

All week long I'd practiced as the first team tight end, a position I'd held since the beginning of the season. When we entered the locker room for a last-minute chalk talk, the last piss, and a chance to say a quick Our Father, Saban announced a line-up change. Andre White would start at tight end.

I was crushed. Here I was appearing before my adopted hometown audience and my old teammates and I was being benched. I approached Sam Rutigliano, the receiver coach, and asked why I wasn't playing. I'd even run dummy plays with the first unit just before we'd come in to put on our pads.

"I didn't like the way you were warming up," he said.

With both teams playing like preschoolers, we lost our fourth in a row, 10-6. Our offense managed only 125 yards in total offense, and the Oilers scored the game's only touchdown on an interception return by Miller Farr. We simply made more mistakes than they did.

Our kicking game had us in constant trouble all afternoon. Rick Duncan had been activated and was handling the kick-offs and placements. He missed three or four field goals, and his kick-offs kept landing around the fifteen-yard line. Just before the gun ended the half, he'd attempted a twenty-five-yard field goal and squibbed it so badly that it almost landed in the sideline stands.

During the half-time intermission Saban screamed at Duncan. "If you don't kick the goddamn ball into the end zone you're gonna be out of here tonight!" Rick Duncan's first kick-off of the second half sailed as far as the ten-yard line and, sure enough, within hours he was no longer a Denver Bronco.

•

For two solid hours Saban verbally tore us to shreds on

Tuesday. Everyone was sweating, a forty-man dead heat for the Pit City award. Some guys tried to hide behind bigger players.

"Some of you people won't be with us next year" were Saban's cutting words. "You'll just have to do the best you can. I realize that our talent isn't on a par with some of the teams of the league," he began quietly, and then shouted, *"but you guys are the laughingstock of football!"*

"Gentlemen," he went on, "I guarantee you that this team will be a winner. It will take a while, but I'll take the few of you who are remaining there. The Denver Broncos will not be losers. I won't let you be."

It was that week that George Goeddeke was activated. The rookie offensive guard was one of the more remarkable characters I've met in football, and I honestly believe that it was George who kept the squad sane that year. He was the clown prince of professional football and would do anything to elicit a laugh. He'd imitate all sort of animals — horses, cows, chickens — at the top of his lungs, and I've seen him do forward somersaults in the middle of a crowded bar, a complete flip in the air, and then land on his feet.

Goeddeke hadn't paid for a haircut since the third grade. He's always shaved his head completely bald, like Yul Brynner. The shape of his skull is not unlike that of a loaf of Russian rye, thus inspiring his nickname: "Bread Head."

Bread Head would ride his motorcycle to practice, walk into the meeting room whistling the Notre Dame Fight Song, and constantly cut up in between meetings and practice. I don't know how he did it. Invariably, he reeked of the previous night's booze, yet he still managed to practice harder than anyone else. I suppose he was making up for time lost among the good brothers at Notre Dame, but he spent every evening patronizing the local bistros. The Store and The Place were his home addresses. Goeddeke was the King of Colfax Street.

Still, he not only made it through practice, he did so with hardly any extra exertion. He had the most extraordinary endurance I've ever seen. And to top it all off, he never got hurt. From that week on, he didn't miss a single game until 1972 when he finally had a knee injury.

✳

A month earlier the newspapers had been talking championship along with everyone else. Now they were down on us. Every morning I'd pick up the morning paper to find headlines like PITY THE POOR BRONCOS!, TOP DRAFT CHOICES A BUST, and THE NEW BRONCOS?

Next we faced the 1966 Eastern Division champion Buffalo Bills, Lou Saban's old team. Saban had departed Buffalo with no love lost, and he wanted the game badly. He was up for this one, and so were we; the South Stand Super Fans were on hand en masse, and cheered our every move wildly. We battled them even for the first half and were left trailing by a single point, 3-2, after the first two periods.

We sensed victory. Saban sensed victory. The Bills were overripe and ready for picking. Late in the third quarter we took the ball on our twenty and began a march that ended with fullback Wendell Hayes smashing over from the one for the game's first touchdown. Our victory-starved fans were going wild.

Our defense held the Bills on the ensuing series of downs, forcing them to punt. Ninety seconds later Al Denson outleapt Buffalo defender Booker Edgerson and came down with a pass in the end zone to put us up by thirteen big points. We could feel the four-game losing streak coming to a halt; there was a sense of elation on our bench and in the stands.

The Bills scored a late touchdown, and we got possession of the ball with five minutes left on the clock. The strategy was clear: run a dive here, an off-tackle there, use up the clock, and then have our punter, Bobby Scarpitto, the league's best, boom the ball right out of the stadium. "Scraps" had averaged an incredible forty-six yards per kick the year before; the game seemed to be on ice. How could we possibly blow this one?

We found a way. **1812109**

With fourth and eleven on our own twenty-four, the ball was snapped perfectly to Scarpitto. Then, instead of kicking the ball, he took off. He'd employed this same bit of deception six times in the past three seasons and had picked up the first down all six times. This time the gamble failed, and he was tackled on the thirty.

The fans were astounded. There was a murmur of incomprehensible expletives throughout the stadium. Saban was thunderstruck. *"Scraps."* He stared at his punter. *"How could you do this to me?"*

The defense tried valiantly to stem the tide, but it had clearly turned. The old pros took the ball and methodically ground out the thirty yards, with Keith Lincoln driving in the final four yards for the tying touchdown. Seconds later Mike Mercer kicked the extra point, and we had discovered yet another way to lose a football game.

I could hardly believe it myself. I was still in a trance as I walked to the locker room. I glanced up and saw the South Stand Super Fans still in their seats. They were stunned also.

Losing was beginning to get to the players. There were short tempers and arguments in abundance. After all we'd lost five in a row and things hardly looked promising for the weeks ahead. We had to play San Diego, Kansas City, and Houston in consecutive games.

The Chargers came to town with an undefeated slate. During the week Saban once again juggled the line-up, making five changes on the starting teams. Sam Brunelli, Ray Kubala, and Steve Tensi all took over starting offensive spots, while Rex Mirich replaced Pete Duranko at defensive end and rookie Jimmy Summers took over Goldie Sellers' left cornerback slot.

We jumped out to a quick 7-0 lead when Nemiah Wilson intercepted a John Hadl pass and ran it all the way in for the score. The Chargers seemed to be toying with us as they tied it up shortly thereafter and scored again in the second quarter to lead 14-7 at half time.

In the second half they turned Dickie Post, Lance Alworth, and Gary Garrison loose, and with Hadl passing for 345 yards overall the Chargers rolled over us, 38-21. Our streak was still intact.

During practice that week we scrimmaged. A full, all-out scrimmage, with pads and helmets and tackling and blocking. It was bad enough that we were 1-6 and lodged in last place. Now we were hitting and beating the crap out of each other during the week. No one bitched though. I suppose everyone was too scared to say anything. Saban figured the only way to prepare for the Chiefs was to force us to get mean.

The Chiefs had their usual great team, but they hadn't been playing up to par in '67. Everyone realized that they were ready to explode and just unmercifully beat the shit out of somebody, and we were just praying it wouldn't be us. In sixteen previous meetings, the Broncos had beaten Kansas City exactly once.

After landing at Kansas City's downtown airport, we rode across the Missouri River on the way to the hotel. I felt like a Christian martyr being led into the lion's den. That night Duranko and I dined at The Cock & Bull, a renowned Kansas City steak house. The owners were very gracious to visiting players and put on a terrific feed that seemed to last all night: twenty-six-ounce steaks, the works. I guess they felt sorry for us.

＊

As I scanned the Chiefs roster in the program before the game it seemed that we were sending out boys to fight grown men. They had no less than twenty-three players with five or more years of playing experience. We had three. And we still had twenty rookies on our roster.

The only thing we did right all afternoon was win the coin toss. After that it was all downhill. We made, I believe, every mistake possible in the course of the game. The only way they didn't score was by a safety. The

Chiefs decimated us 52-9, and the game wasn't as close as the score indicated. Had Hank Stram wanted to, Kansas City probably could have run up 100 points.

We fumbled three times in the first half, and the Chiefs turned all three into touchdowns. Midway through the second quarter it was already 35-0, and although we scored once to get on the board on a Tensi-to-Denson fifty-two-yard bomb, Kansas City came back within moments to equalize things with yet another touchdown. They took a 42-7 lead into the locker room at half time. I was scared to death. We were about to be wiped off the face of the earth, and I was absolutely powerless to do anything about it. It was hopeless.

Saban didn't say a word in the locker room. He was wrung out. There was no half-time strategy talk. Xs and Os on a blackboard were not going to save us. The coaches walked out and left us alone in the locker room. We gathered together and vowed to play the game out if for no other reason than our pride as men. We'd already been thoroughly embarrassed. Now we were fighting for more than just our jobs.

We played a little better in the second half, but Hank Stram helped us save no inconsiderable degree of face by keeping the ball on the ground and playing his reserves for the rest of the game. As I watched the seconds tick off on the scoreboard clock, I never realized that football could be so painful.

There was dead silence on the plane all the way back to Denver. When we had landed and were walking through the terminal, two elderly ladies walking in front of me couldn't imagine who we were. After some speculation the older of the two turned to me and asked, "Pardon me, young man, are you by any chance the Colorado University Glee Club?"

*

Oh God, I thought on Tuesday. Another Tuesday meeting. It's amazing how quickly Tuesdays rolled around in Denver. By this time some of the guys were close to the edge and about to be pushed off. They knew it. Saban crucified us. "You people," he screamed, "are stealing money from the Denver Bronco organization. I shouldn't even be paying you for this sort of performance. You owe me money. And some of you," he added, "won't have to worry about signing contracts for next year. You'll be out of here by December eighteenth. Worms."

You could have heard an eyelash blink.

When he showed the game films he kept stopping the projector and running it back when the camera caught the scoreboard: 42-7, 42-7, 42-7, 42-7, 42-7. It was ridiculous. Then 52-9, 52-9, 52-9, 52-9 — over and over. I wanted to hide somewhere.

*

And now we had to prepare for the Oakland Raiders again. They'd beaten us 51-0 and were just coming off a 51-10 stomping of the San Diego Chargers, a team that had also manhandled us. The local sportswriters were picking us to lose by anywhere from thirty to sixty points, give or take a safety.

Before practice on Tuesday, center Dave Behrman paused while pulling on his jersey and said, "Just think. The season is more than halfway over." It seemed as if we'd been playing for an eternity.

The Raiders arrived in Denver cocky and arrogant, expecting us, I suppose, to roll over and play dead. For a change, we didn't.

The weather proved a boon for us. Two days before the game a foot of snow had fallen on Denver, and the Californians weren't fond of cold weather. Our defense held the powerful Oakland running attack in check, but the difference in the game was the Raider defense. Their infamous 5-2 stacked formation caused no end of problems for us. Our quarterbacks were sacked eleven times for ninety-five yards. You don't win football games with that sort of statistic. Ben Davidson, Ike Lassiter, Dan Birdwell, Tom Keating, and Carleton Oats poured into our backfield all afternoon.

We lost the game 21-17, but most of us considered it a moral victory at least. Maybe, we were thinking, just maybe this signaled the end of the streak. Then, as I walked down the runway leading to the locker room, I heard an inebriated fan shout, "I want to congratulate you guys. You just broke the record for the most consecutive losses."

As we continued to plummet toward the depths of oblivion, some of the players began to seek diversions to keep their minds off football. Bo Hickey and Tom Cichowski would get up at five or six in the morning to go hunting before coming to practice. Larry Kaminski and Mike Current enjoyed fishing. A lot of players, though, sought refuge in a friend named John Barleycorn, and not a few guys were hitting the bottle rather heavily in an effort to escape what had happened to us.

We had a tough week of practice in preparation for the Houston game, hoping to halt our "record" in its tracks. The Oilers, like seemingly everyone else we were playing, were enjoying a winning season.

Once again there were major changes in the starting line-ups. Center Dave Behrman, fullback Wendell Hayes, tackle Ray Kubala, and linebackers Chip Myrtle and Carl Cunningham were all benched.

We did play better than we had in our first encounter with the Oilers. So did they. We lost number nine, 20-18. I was beginning to wonder whether I was a born masochist. It was hard to believe that ten weeks before we'd been undefeated and leading our division.

*

With the rematch against the Bills in Buffalo coming up, a genuine Rocky Mountain blizzard hit Denver in midweek, covering the practice field with snow. It was funny to watch Don Smith and Andre White, two rookies from Florida A & M who'd never seen snow, as they rolled about and cavorted, throwing snow balls at everyone else. They were like kids with a new toy. Practicing in a foot of snow, though, is something else. Everyone had his own means of staying warm.

All the players except Goeddeke wore thermal underwear. The hardest parts of the body to keep warm were the hands and feet. Most of the guys wore gloves, a luxury denied to the receivers and backs. The soggy, frozen football weighed a ton. It was like trying to catch a brick, and the quarterbacks, unable to grip the ball properly, were throwing up more wounded ducks and flutterballs than spirals. Since football shoes aren't waterproof, some guys would wrap plastic cleaning bags around their shoes and then tape the whole shoe, coating the tape with Vaseline.

This form of footwarming was short-lived. One player wrapped his feet too tightly and, cutting off the circulation, had to be carried off the field. Other players took to wearing galoshes over sneakers. Andre White would try to run a pass pattern in his galoshes and run out of gas before the ball was thrown. It was like running with lead weights on each foot.

And of course there were daily snowball fights and other antics like shoving snow down somebody's freezing ass, under his jersey, or between the air holes on the side of his helmet. Lots of fun. Then there was another day when flanker Eric Crabtree took off on a corner pattern. Tensi lofted a high, arching floater. Looking back over his shoulder, Crabtree ran straight into a six-foot snowbank at the end of the field. Several seconds later he emerged looking like a black snowman.

But the weather did prep us for Buffalo. Buffalo in November is like the North and South Poles combined. Ice, sleet, snow, and cold. All at the same time. The day before the game it had snowed eight inches, most of which had melted by game time. The field looked like the Ho Chi Minh Trail at the height of the monsoon season — nothing but mud.

The groundskeepers had poured some sort of drying agent on the turf to try to make the field playable, and the stuff smelled like week-old vomit.

We know how much Saban wanted to win in front of the Buffalo crowd. He always did.

We played a good football game and led for fifty-nine minutes and twenty-four seconds before oblivion once again stared us directly in the face. We'd had the ball first and ten on the Buffalo forty-nine, leading 21-20. On the first play from scrimmage, Bo Hickey fumbled and the Bills recovered. We had apparently devised yet another means of throwing away a game.

Buffalo quarterback (and now U.S. Congressman) Jack Kemp took the Buffalo offense and began to move it in a piecemeal fashion. Four yards here, five there. The clock continued to run, and then with thirty-six seconds left the Bills called a time out with the ball on our sixteen.

Mike Mercer, who had already kicked two field goals — including one from the forty-three — trotted out to kick the chip shot. I couldn't bear to watch.

I shut my eyes tightly, and the next thing I heard was a groan from the crowd. Players were jubilantly jumping up and down and cheering on our bench. Mercer had squibbed the kick! We'd broken the losing streak at nine. We celebrated in the locker room. What a relief! It felt so good to win a game that no one seemed to mind, when we pulled off our mud-caked uniforms, that there was only one shower working and no hot water in the joint. For once Tuesday morning would be a long time arriving.

*

We had three games remaining, all against winning teams — the Chargers, Jets, and Chiefs. On Thanksgiving Day we handed the game to San Diego when Speedy Duncan ran a blocked field goal all the way back for a touchdown to beat us, 24-20. At least when we were losing games, though, we were losing them by respectable scores. And there were only two games left to play. It was mathematically impossible, at least this year, to run up another nine-game losing skein.

*

We arrived in New York to play the Eastern Division–leading Jets. Namath and his mates had only to beat or tie two of their last four opponents to win the Eastern Division, and we were considered such easy prey that, word had it, Namath had been out all night celebrating his team's victory. He was somewhat premature.

Reserve Mike Kellogg set the tempo for things to come when, on the opening kick-off, he raced downfield and flew into the middle of the Jet wedge feet first.

We scored twenty-six points, a team record, in the second quarter, while our defense blanked the Jets. Joe Willie tried to rally the New Yorkers and threw for three touchdown passes in the second half but to no avail. We scored another touchdown in the third period to give us the margin of victory. Our secondary intercepted Namath (who threw sixty passes during the game) four times. It really *was* "the greatest victory in Bronco history."

Most of the guys were half smashed before they got in the air, and the trip back was sublime insanity. It had been a big win. I remember that at some point in flight, Coach Saban walked to the rear of the plane. Standing in the midst of the celebrants, he confidently said, "Keep improving. I'll get you there."

In our last game we fell to the Chiefs, 38-24. We'd come, at least, a long way from 52-9. We all breathed a sigh of relief that it was over at last.

Tomorrow would be a new day, a new season, a new lease on life. We had nowhere to go but up and hoped that within a few short months 1967 would be a nightmare faded from memory.

5

Limeys, Magicians, and Lou: Babylon Revisited

I STAYED IN DENVER another two years, and conditions didn't improve much. We'd win one and lose three. Tuesdays were about the same. The only consolation came in the fact that we managed to avoid those agonizing losing streaks, and on the whole I suppose we were playing better football. So, unfortunately, was our opposition.

Training camp was training camp. Fatigue, six weeks of feeling like dog shit after being pressed through two-a-days, and, as is always the case when you're playing for a lousy team, a few hundred bodies passed in and out of camp. While we labored under Saban's version of the Chinese water torture, someone with infinite foresight scheduled one of our 1968 exhibition games for San Antonio. Talk about survival of the fittest! If you can live through four quarters of football in San Antonio in August you feel like you've just stood off Santa Anna's army.

Rather than pay for an extra night's rent, the team arranged to have us check out of the hotel at three in the afternoon. The game was scheduled for eight that night. The entire squad — I think there were fifty or sixty of us left by then — had to mill around the esplanade and mall outside for two and a half hours in the sweltering heat while we waited for the buses. When they finally arrived on the scene we were crammed inside and driven to something called Alamo Stadium, constructed roughly at the same time they built the Roman Colosseum, and then literally herded — if the coaches had been armed with cattle prods I wouldn't have blinked — into a minuscule locker room devoid of air conditioning.

Presumably the San Diego club had been provided with similar accommodations, because in a tremendous offensive clash we lost to the Chargers, 6-3. The game marked the beginning of the end for our new place kicker, Jack Abendschan, a former Canadian League superstar who was trying to hook on with the Broncos. With several opportunities from short range, Abendschan managed to kick footballs everywhere but through the uprights.

The next weekend we played our final exhibition game in Portland, Oregon, against our old friends the Raiders, and even though it was a meaningless preseason game Saban desperately wanted to win. The game was played in Multnomah Stadium, which had one end zone built right into the side of a steep hill. Rising from the hill was a sort of combination hotel-geriatric ward, with a bunch of old folks rocking and dozing, dozing and rocking on the balcony. I kept thinking about how comfortable they seemed.

We should have let the old folks play the Raiders, because with Lamonica throwing three TD passes we lost, 23-7. Abendschan missed a few more field goals and it was goodbye.

❖

But at least the exhibitions were over and done with. The next weekend in Cincinnati we proceeded to make NFL history by becoming the first club ever to be beaten by an expansion team on opening day. The Bengals, a hopeless conglomerate of free agents, rookies, misfits, rejects, has-beens, and guys who'd been waived out of the Atlantic Coast League, soundly stomped us, 24-10.

In many ways it was like an exhibition game, beginning with the fact that it was played at Nippert Stadium, the home field of the University of Cincinnati, and somehow when you're playing against guys with names like Saint Saffold, Estes Banks, and Dewey "Swamp Rat" Warren you don't feel like you're playing a real football team.

They were real enough though. Moreover, we were soundly outcoached. Paul Brown made the most of his rag-tag outfit and combined a very stubborn defense with all sorts of razzle-dazzle plays on offense. Meanwhile, we couldn't do anything right.

Our quarterback, John McCormick, subbing for the injured Tensi, had failed to generate even a semblance of offense, and midway through the third period Saban had given him the hook in favor of Jim LeClair, a rookie from C. W. Post. LeClair couldn't do anything with the offense either, but he did manage to provide one of the game's highlights late in the quarter. We were deep in our own territory when LeClair called a pass play. He faded back with the snap, set himself in the pocket, cocked, and fired. As he threw he lost his grip on the ball and it went sailing straight back over his head and bounced crazily toward our goal line. We did recover the ball — albeit for a twenty-yard loss —

but only because the Bengals were so startled that they just sort of stood there and looked around for the phantom receiver. Perhaps Paul Brown had that one in the Cincinnati playbook. I know it wasn't in ours. The play merited a spot on the weekly highlights of NFL blunders on "The Tonight Show." Quite an honor for us.

As we walked off the field I stole a glance at Saban. His face was a vivid purple. So was his prose. If words could kill we'd have all been goners. I put my head down and kept walking.

•

The Tuesday meeting was what you might expect. McCormick, who'd started the game at quarterback Sunday, showed up and sat quietly through the general meeting. When the team broke up for individual meetings, McCormick was locked out of the room where the offensive backs met. He knocked a couple of times, and finally Hunter Enis, the offensive backfield coach, stuck his head out the door and told John not to bother coming in. I guess the coaches hadn't informed the quarterback that they had put him on waivers that morning.

Our whole offensive situation was grim. We had three untried rookie quarterbacks, LeClair, "Colfax" Joe DiVito of Boston College, and Alan Pastrana of Maryland, and for all intents and purposes no place kicker. The next week we lost to the Chiefs in Kansas City by a score of 34 to 2. You don't have to know much about football to realize that you can't win if you can't score.

But just as we were boarding the bus from the stadium to

the K.C. airport, a balding, middle-aged man with a British accent approached Saban and asked him for a tryout. He was, he explained, a soccer-style kicker whom Hank Stram had recruited from one of his European talent contests the previous spring. Unfortunately for him, the Chiefs also had a guy named Jan Stenerud in camp that year, and Stenerud eventually won the job.

We were in such desperate shape that I suspect Saban would have given Lizzie Borden a tryout if she'd asked, but when he invited Bobby Howfield back to Denver that week it proved to be one of the smartest moves the man ever made. The limey, it turned out, could kick.

As we practiced for our home opener against the Boston Patriots that week, Tensi was still on the mend, DiVito and Pastrana were gone. Saban installed an obscure defensive back named Marlin Briscoe as back-up to LeClair. A rookie, Briscoe had been a Little All-American at Omaha. He was also black, and never in the history of the National Football League had a black quarterback participated in a regular season game.

Nearly 40,000 people showed up for the game, many of them to see Briscoe. The curiosity inspired by the possibility of actually seeing a black quarterback evidently appealed to the conservative Denverites.

LeClair started, and although the score was 10-10 at half time he wasn't having what you'd call a good day. He was three for thirteen for thirty-one yards for the half. Midway through the fourth period the Patriots had run up a 20 to 10 lead when Saban gave Briscoe the word to warm up for the next series.

It was instant electricity. The whole place went crazy as history was made. Marlin the Magician, as he was instantly tabbed by the media, took our inept offense and somehow moved us. With 2:53 left he hit Billy Van Heusen for a twenty-yard gain, and then an interference call gave us a first down on the Patriot thirty-one. With time running out Briscoe took the ball, rolled out to pass, and took off. He gained nineteen yards for a first down at the twelve. Then he regrouped us at the line of scrimmage and called a play. It was totally alien. Not only was it not one of the six plays they'd had Marlin learn, it wasn't even in our playbook. The quizzical linemen were asking each other what they were supposed to do, and the backs didn't know where to line up. Then, at the snap, Briscoe took the ball and ran like hell, dodging tacklers and scampering into the end zone for the score. Suddenly we were in the game with one minute left. We got the ball back with forty seconds left, but we were out of time outs. The clock ran out before Marlin could get us in again, but there wasn't a soul in the place who doubted that with enough time he would have.

I felt proud to have been a part of Marlin's debut. In just six minutes of playing time he'd gained fifty-one yards rushing and passed for another forty-three. Ninety-four yards total offense on the day didn't seem bad for a kid who was only supposed to know six plays.

Briscoe was naturally the focus of attention in the locker room, as the reporters congregated around him. A star had been born. At the other end of the room sat the dejected figure of Bobby Howfield. He'd missed two of three field-goal attempts, including a twenty-four-yarder late in the game. "I let the chaps down between the posts," Bobby said. "And between the posts is the nyme of the gyme."

You bet your ass it is, I was thinking. If history was a precedent, I figured Howfield had exactly one week to redeem himself or he'd be back in the Mother Country by Guy Fawkes Day.

The press, TV, and radio people converged on our practice field in north Denver all week as we prepared for the rematch with the Bengals. It was unbelievable. Here we were, 0-3 and going nowhere, and suddenly all this attention was being lavished upon us both nationally and locally.

The reason, of course, was Marlin Briscoe. He certainly had earned the attention he was getting. He is a truly great athlete, but suddenly the local writers decided that he could also perform miracles.

Before a record crowd, Briscoe started against Cincinnati, but this time his inexperience showed. Paul Brown had installed a defense that had him thoroughly rattled and confused. The Bengals blitzed on every passing down, and Brown had a couple of defenders keying on Briscoe in running situations. Marlin never did get untracked, and we were down 7-0 at half time.

Tensi had been activated during the week, and at the start of the second half he replaced Briscoe, and with the defense shutting the Bengals out for the rest of the game we won, 10-7. Now suddenly Tensi was the man of the hour, and while the gentlemen of the press swarmed around his locker, Marlin Briscoe quietly dressed alone.

Howfield had kicked a thirty-four-yard field goal that eventually proved to be the margin of victory. "I sye, myte," he gleefully chortled, "I had a rather spiffy boot, now didn't I." Spiffy, all right, I thought. If he'd missed it he might still be hanging by his bloody neck from the goal post.

✽

When we flew to New York to play the Jets the next week, we did so without our star flanker, Eric Crabtree. He was AWOL, and nobody knew where he was. He finally showed up at the hotel Saturday night, and then the next day went out and caught five passes for 148 yards, including the game-winning touchdown, as we beat the Jets in the Big Apple. Suddenly we were 2-3. One game under .500. The plane trip back was total insanity; you'd have thought we'd just won the Super Bowl. We were swilling champagne by the case in the midst of a cacophony of triumphant voices. It was Saban's birthday, which he further celebrated by leading us in a rousing rendition of "Happy Birthday, Dear Lou," and of course the happiest guy on the plane was Crabtree. He'd not only played a fantastic game, but in one of his more magnanimous gestures, Saban had rescinded the normally automatic fine for missing the team plane.

There was a crowd of over a thousand frenzied fans waiting to greet our plane when we arrived back in Denver. Some of us were so hammered we had to be led off the plane and quietly ushered into limousines so the locals wouldn't see us staggering around.

✽

In San Diego the next week Tensi was reinjured halfway through the second quarter and had to be carried off the field. Suddenly it was once again all up to Marlin, and what a show he put on! Against the second-best defense in the AFL he made believers out of everybody. In the two and a half quarters he played, Briscoe passed for 237 yards and three touchdowns, and in five carries he picked up another sixty-eight on the ground. Although the Chargers offense massacred us, once again Briscoe was the darling of the media.

But with Tensi recovering during the week Lou decided to go with experience and started Steve again the next Sunday against the Dolphins. Over 44,000 fans had come to see Marlin the Magician, and Tensi never had a chance. They were on his back from the opening kick-off, and partly because we hadn't gone anywhere during the first half and partly in response to the crowd, Saban went to Briscoe at the beginning of the second half.

There was near pandemonium in the stands, and Briscoe responded by starting to move us from a 14-0 half-time deficit. He slithered through the Miami secondary for twelve yards and our first touchdown, moved us to another, and late in the fourth quarter, with the game tied 14-14 and a Bronco first down on the Dolphins' ten, we broke the huddle and Marlin looked over the Miami defense.

"Two, Two, Two," he barked out the signal. I almost fell over. Linemen were looking at each other, wondering if Briscoe had taken leave of his senses. He'd checked off to a quarterback sneak! On first and ten?

He took the snap and was gone like a shot. I swear to God nobody laid a hand on him. The Dolphins were more startled than we were. Mile High Stadium exploded.

Talk about black magic! In just two quarters Marlin the Magician had scored two touchdowns and racked up 143 yards in total offense in turning a hopelessly lost cause into what was not just a win but a personal triumph of the first magnitude.

But, inexplicably, Saban continued to use Briscoe only sporadically for the balance of the season, which proved to be a decided mediocrity, as he stuck with the more experienced Tensi. Without taking anything away from Steve, who was a decent quarterback himself, Briscoe had played fantastically, and like they say, when you're hot, you're hot. A lot of players, myself included, couldn't understand why Marlin wasn't the number one quarterback.

*

Later that season we were playing the Bills in Denver, and at one point in the game we had run up such a massive lead we were threatening to blow them off the field and all the way back to Buffalo. Then, in typical Bronco fashion, we began to piss the game away in a barrage of miscues. A fumble here, an interception there, and suddenly we were only leading 31-29. On second down and with a little more than a minute to go in the game, Floyd Little took a hand-off and tried to circumnavigate the left end. He was hit, fumbled, and Buffalo's George Saimes picked up the ball and was streaking for the end zone. Floyd caught him at the twelve, and rather than run the clock down, which seemed the rational thing to do, the Bills elected to kick a field goal on first down.

We were in a daze. After leading 31-14 we were behind

32-31. Sheer panic swept our bench. Everything was in a state of utter chaos as players and coaches ran around in circles. Nobody had the slightest idea of what to do. Saban was screaming that if we lost the game everybody on the team would be on waivers Monday morning. The tone in his voice indicated that he was not kidding.

The kick-off return team looked for Lou to ask for instructions. He was nowhere to be found. The officials were insisting that we take the field and nobody could find the coach.

Suddenly I spotted him. He was down on the ground on all fours pounding his fists into the turf and pulling up fistfuls of sod. He was raging. He definitely would have liked to kill every last one of us.

We returned the kick-off to our own twenty-seven, with thirty seconds showing on the clock. Little, having set up Buffalo's go-ahead field goal, wanted to atone for his sin. In the huddle he asked Briscoe to throw him the ball. The two of them knelt down and devised, on the spot, a play in the turf, just like in sandlot football. Briscoe would roll left, stop, and throw the ball a mile to Little.

Marlin took the ball, rolled, stopped, rolled again, and threw a long spiral to Floyd. It must have traveled almost seventy yards in the air. Bobby Howfield raced onto the field and kicked a field goal with a couple of seconds left. Saban very nearly had a coronary. I was just thinking, "Thank God we won," because the unemployment line is long on Monday mornings.

❋

Nineteen sixty-eight ended 5-9, and we looked forward to
'69 with a "wait until next year" attitude. For Marlin Briscoe it was a year to remember. Even though he had passed
for fourteen touchdowns and racked up almost 2000 yards in
total offense, and made the AFL All-Rookie team, Marlin
the Magician would never again wear the orange and blue
of the Denver Broncos. My own view is that his performance in '68 won't be matched by a rookie quarterback for a
long time to come.

Briscoe was notified that he would be playing cornerback
in 1969 and the gifted quarterback objected. He was
quickly shuffled off to Buffalo. Saban had to go with Tensi.
He gave up too much to keep him on the bench.

❋

Nineteen sixty-nine proved to be a season equally rich in fu-
tility. The highlight of the year had to be the last day of
two-a-day workouts. (It was the most interesting afternoon
in Denver since the year before, when linebacker Gordie
Lambert, in full equipment, was served with his divorce papers on the practice field.) We had just been through seven
weeks of camp, and on the final day, a sweltering summer
afternoon, a truck drove right up onto the practice field. As
tough as Lou Saban was, he did take care of his players, and
in this case the truck was loaded with beer. The Coors was
like gold to us. Players milled around the truck for hours.
It was the only time I ever stayed around for two hours after
practice. The shower sobered me up just enough to crawl
home.

The exhibition season was long and costly. We defeated

the '49ers in a war of attrition that saw us lose four players to knee surgery. I think that still stands as an NFL record. Another time we played an exhibition game in Jacksonville in ninety-five-degree heat. As we filed out onto the field for warm-ups, George Goeddeke looked up and noticed Bobby Howfield sitting in the stands, fully dressed in his uniform. He was sitting with some friends, joking and eating a hot dog.

Howfield was irrepressible. He always shaved before games, while other players were tense and nervous and pacing and fidgeting around the locker room in a deathly sort of silence. Then all of a sudden you'd hear Howfield belt out a few verses of "The ryne in Spyne styes mynely on the plyne." He was very fortunate that some uptight lineman didn't slit his throat. Bobby had also showed up for camp that summer with his body shaved. He said he wanted to get a better tan. The guy was whacky as hell, but he was a fine chap, an endless beer drinker, and one heck of a kicker.

*

Marlin Briscoe thought that after his '68 showing he should be offered a chance to play quarterback, but during the winter Saban had acquired a Canadian League phenom named Pete Liske. Liske had been a CFL All-Star at Winnipeg, and, locker room rumor had it, had signed with the Broncos for half the Denver mint. Saban must have wanted him pretty badly, reasoning that Tensi was injury-prone and Briscoe inexperienced.

We'd gotten through the exhibition season in splendid mediocrity, but somehow when the games were for real we put it all together. For a while. We won our first two games, including a 21-19 victory over Joe Namath and the Jets. Not to be outdone, Joe Willie White Shoes passed for nearly 300 yards that afternoon. The stadium was packed with people who'd come to see Namath, and the city of Denver was all but deserted. People who didn't have tickets packed up and left for Cheyenne, North Platte, and Rapid City to escape the blackout and watch the game on television.

It was as spectacular a game as they could have hoped for. They say you can kick a ball a mile in the thin atmosphere of Denver. That afternoon the Jets' Steve O'Neal almost did — ninety-eight yards for an NFL record. Our locker roon afterward was sheer bedlam, and Saban, sensing the light at the end of the tunnel, was grinning from ear to ear. It was the first time in the history of the Denver Broncos that the team had been undefeated after two games, and we'd just knocked off the Super Bowl champs at that. Lou led the team in prayer after the game and said that it was our biggest win ever. It was our time to make a move.

*

We flew to Buffalo to play the winless Bills. Their whole club was ripe with dissension. Players were openly criticizing the coach, John Rauch. Marlin, playing wide receiver for the Bills, muttered, "And I thought Denver was bad." The Buffalo press was crapping all over the organization. They were having all sorts of quarterback problems, and the fans were up in arms because of Rauch's minimal use of O. J.

Simpson, who had been employed largely as a decoy for their first two games.

Being the Denver Broncos, though, we reverted to form. Although we led 14 to 3 at the end of the first period, the Bills proceeded to intercept Liske five times and run over us, 41-28. Saban was furious. The Buffalo fans had given him a tremendous ovation before the game, remembering the bygone days when Lou had led the Bills to championships. With Buffalo on a twelve-game losing streak — which we snapped for them — the crowd was cheering for us more than the Bills. Lou had really wanted that one.

With Kansas City and Oakland next on the agenda, those play-off dollars were already starting to fade from view. Then on Friday night before the K.C. game, the skies darkened and the temperature fell to below freezing. It started snowing. And snowing. A goddamn blizzard on October 3? Saturday's practice was canceled because most of the players couldn't dig their cars out of the snow, which was by then knee-deep.

It snowed right up until Sunday morning. Guys who lived up in the foothills were stranded, and several got to the stadium only a few minutes before game time. The stadium crew had put in sixty-six hours trying to get the field into shape, to no avail. It was a quagmire of ankle-deep mud.

The effect on our offense was disastrous. We couldn't run, the receivers couldn't make cuts, and when we did we couldn't catch the ball anyway. Those big monsters like Aaron Brown and Buck Buchanan just dug their cleats into the soggy turf and rushed like hell. The outcome was never in doubt.

The situation was returning to normalcy very quickly. Nobody was talking about play-offs anymore with league-leading Oakland coming to town. They say that lightning doesn't strike twice. Wrong again. On Friday the skies darkened. And the temperatures dropped. And the goddamn snow started falling. And falling.

The city of Denver was in a panic. It was still early autumn, and the trees still had leaves. There was a 50 percent loss of trees and foliage in Denver, with huge glazed limbs snapping and falling into the streets and across power lines.

More deleterious still was the effect on the field. It was so cold that this time the field froze over into a solid sheet of ice. One week you play in a swamp, the next on a hockey rink.

The fans had a field day, throwing snowballs and sipping brandy, and while we acquitted ourselves well, the Raiders played better. We were not blown out of the game, and we played them pretty evenly. Unfortunately, a blocked punt cost us the game. Three short weeks before we'd been sitting on top of the world and now we were in last place.

The balance of the season was comprised of a whole succession of typical Broncoisms. We'd win one, lose two, the same old shit. I was, though, afforded the opportunity to join that not-so-exclusive NFL club, the Gnarled Knees. It was my first knee injury, but not my last.

I'd heard through the grapevine that at least one Bronco coach harbored a desire to get me the hell out of town. I wasn't what they call a burner — a guy with sensational speed — and I suppose he had visions of coming up with a Charley Sanders or a Bob Trumpy to replace me. In any case, after the knee injury I had a feeling my days in the Rocky Mountains were numbered. Saban was openly airing his intention to "make changes." We needed more offense, sure, and drafted Bobby Anderson of Colorado on the first round that winter.

Even the fans were beginning to sour on us. While we still sold out every game, the crowds were becoming more antagonistic and openly hostile as their patience dwindled. The fan reaction began to take its toll on the management, and while the press in Denver wasn't exactly hostile like, say, the writers in Boston, New York, or Philadelphia, where controversy is the number one priority, after three losing seasons and a combined 13-28-1 record the Denver scribes were beginning to question Saban's methods. "You don't need a weatherman to know which way the wind is blowing," like the man said. The inevitable was bound to happen.

It did. Early in April I was working out at the Broncos' practice field in north Denver when I got a call from Fred Gehrke, the player personnel director. At first I figured he wanted to talk about renewing my contract. He didn't.

"Tom," he told me, "I've got some bad news for you." Possibilities leapt to mind. Detroit? Had I been traded back to the old hometown? Houston? The old college stomping grounds? *Anywhere* where they win football games?

"We have," he went on, "traded you to Boston for Jim Whalen."

"Jesus Christ," I thought to myself. "What the hell kind of trade is *that*? A tight end for a tight end?"

I remembered something Saban had said earlier in the year. "The Denver Broncos are *not* the last stop in the NFL any longer. You can always go to Boston or Buffalo."

The Boston Patriots. We'd kicked their butts 35 to 7 the previous season. Kicked their tails, yet, in a game in which Saban had ordered us to keep the ball on the ground after we'd run it up to 28-0 in the first half.

All I knew about the Patriots was that they were terrible, they didn't have a stadium, and they had very little fan support. I remember also thinking about leaving the Rockies and the fresh air in order to go to the East Coast and choke to death.

I sat there for a minute and let it sink in. I realized that I was just about to enter into an entirely new ball game. My intuition, it turned out, was absolutely correct. The Boston Patriots did indeed march to a different drummer.

6

Becoming an
Improper Bostonian

I LEFT DENVER with mixed emotions. I hated leaving the Rockies, I hated the thought of not being around those football-crazed Bronco fans. I even felt bad about leaving Lou Saban. I respected him while I was simultaneously scared to death of the man, but I felt the trade meant he had given up on me. I'd done my best, but I guess he didn't think that was good enough.

I wished him the best though, loaded up my car, and purchased a couple of six-packs of Coors for the road east.

I stopped in Detroit en route to visit my parents, and one day a message arrived. There had been a rumbling of war drums between the NFL owners and the players' association. This time it was for real. The telegram was signed by our president, John Mackey, and it asked all NFL players to remain away from our summer training sites. A strike was on.

Talk about a breath of springtime! The next day my dad and I loaded up his car and headed for the summer house in Upper Michigan. I'd listen to the radio every day, and each evening I'd hear the good news: "No end in sight in NFL player-owner dispute; both parties sticking to their guns." What that meant was more fishing, more sun, and no damn two-a-days.

The situation began to grow critical after the first week though. For one thing, I wasn't making any money fishing. For another, the exhibition season was fast approaching. Preseason games mean money for veteran players, and my finances were depleted. Finally word came across the air waves that Pete Rozelle had called for arbitration. It was time to leave for home.

A few days later I got a call from the Patriots player rep, Houston Antwine, telling me that the strike was over and we had three days to report.

*

I drove across Ontario and New York State, and then I saw that huge green sign welcoming me to New England. The last time I'd been in New England was when we'd beaten the shit out of the Patriots, 35-14. Now I was one of them.

I reported to the camp on the campus of the University of Massachusetts in Amherst. After checking in at the field house I headed for a pub called Chequers, with which I would become very familiar before camp ended. It was the official pub of the Pats.

I ran into several veteran Patriots there, Mike Montler, Tommy Neville, Len St. Jean, and Jon Morris among them. I listened for the most part as they discussed my new team, and then they began to quiz me about life with the Broncos.

Was Saban as tough as people said he was? How hard were Denver's workouts?

After I'd answered their queries the consensus among the Patriot players was that they were damned fortunate to be in Boston. One guy told me that he'd be thoroughly surprised if two-a-days lasted more than two weeks in Amherst. Others told me about eighty-minute workouts, frequently without pads. A third player assured me that the team seldom hit or scrimmaged.

I was in a state of shock in the face of these revelations. I had become accustomed to getting my head beaten in by Rich "Tombstone" Jackson and Pete Duranko on more-or-less a daily basis. Another player chimed in and told me that if the team had to run sprints everyone bitched like hell. No sprints? No scrimmages? No pads? Practices over at 1:00 P.M.? I wasn't going to a football team, I was thinking, I was going to a country club.

*

When practice commenced the next day I learned that what I'd heard in the pub was true. It was a living dream. I sensed that I was getting out of shape, and there was no way I was going to stay in condition that way. I hung around after practice and ran on my own.

The team itself had some excellent football players. Jim Nance, Jon Morris, 1969 AFL Rookie of the Year Carl Garrett, and kicker Gino Cappelletti were legitimate stars. The defense featured the "Molemen," Houston Antwine and Jimmy Hunt. I remembered at Denver how the offensive linemen had botched up every time they'd had to face the

Boston Moles. I think they'd have preferred going against Kansas City's Buck Buchanan and Ernie Ladd than Antwine and Hunt, both of whom were extremely tough and very quick off the ball.

Training camp itself was a breeze. Believe it or not, we only had three days of double sessions. The new coach, Clive Rush, had been an assistant with the New York Jets, and he believed in running the camp the way the Jets ran theirs, i.e., very loosely. The fastest anyone ran all summer was when they happened to be sneaking out the back door of the dormitory after the 11:00 P.M. curfew.

The exhibition season was a change of pace. Among the garden spots we were scheduled to visit were Jackson, Mississippi, and Shreveport, Louisiana. Our first game, though, was played at Boston College, against the Redskins. The game itself was fairly exciting, with the Vince Lombardi–less Washington club leading by two touchdowns. Then all of a sudden I noticed the fans running around madly, pouring out of the bleachers behind our bench by the hundreds. Then, I was startled to notice, there were huge flames leaping up into the sky. The stands were on fire! Meanwhile, the game was still going on. The people had a choice of watching the Redskins burn us or the fire burn down the stadium.

Most of them opted for the fire. Finally, with the fire engines approaching the stadium, the referees signaled time out. The players gathered on their field and watched the firemen set about their work. The fans naturally poured out onto the field and mingled with the players as we waited for the blaze to be extinguished. Kids were getting autographs and players' wives came out to stand alongside their padded husbands. When the blaze was finally put out they resumed the game. It was without doubt the best half-time show I've ever seen. How many teams, after all, are willing to burn down the stands for the entertainment of the fans?

◦

The game against the Saints in Jackson was singularly unmemorable, and the trip would have been best forgotten had it not been for a couple of things that happened before we even set foot on the field. First the bus broke down taking the team to the hotel. The team filed out and, after cooperating in an effort to push it off the road, we had to hitchhike, catch as catch can, to the hotel on our own.

Later that evening I was in a taxi on my way back to the hotel when I noticed a strange apparition ahead of me. I couldn't believe it, but the closer I got the more I realized that my eyes hadn't deceived me. There, driving in the opposite lane on the highway, was our quarterback, Mike Taliaferro. He was steering down the road in a golf cart.

The next stop on our tour of the sunny south was Shreveport. Since the opponent was the Steelers, the rationale was that the game should draw well; their quarterback, Terry Bradshaw, is a Shreveport native. I'm still not sure how many fans showed up for the game. We had other things on our minds.

After dressing at the Ramada Inn we took a bus to the Fairgrounds. The stadium is normally used for rodeos or 4-H Club shows, but in any case the facilities were so atrocious that most of the guys wouldn't even use the latrines. The floor was covered with an inch or so of water, or what we supposed was water, and floating atop the liquid were curious little lumps of matter. No one was sure what they were, but the first thing that crossed everyone's mind was naturally that there were turds floating around the john.

Now, since this was, after all, the Fairgrounds, speculation immediately leapt to mind: 'What *kind* of shit was it. I mean, it could have been horse, cow, or pig shit. It might have even been sheep dung or, for that matter, redneck turds. Whatever it was, nobody was overanxious to find out, and, playing like some manner of crap ourselves, we lost, 31-3.

*

Something had gone awry in virtually every outing. Our final exhibition was against my old friends, the Denver Broncos, in Salt Lake City. We arrived early at the airport for a scheduled four-and-a-half-hour flight, and on boarding the plane I had my first encounter with the legendary Jim Nance. One of the all-time leading rushers in the old AFL, Nance had held out for an astronomical contract before finally coming to terms with Patriots president Billy Sullivan, who made no bones about the fact that Nance was now one of the highest-paid athletes in professional sports — possibly to counteract his own reputation for penury. Nance had reported "happy and ready to play." Unfortunately, as was his wont, he was also twenty pounds overweight.

While the stewardesses passed out soft drinks, we waited for the mechanics to repair some sort of "minor electrical difficulties." Two hours later we were finally cleared for takeoff, but as the jet kicked over its engines and started barreling down the runway a violent vibration set in toward the rear of the aircraft. Players were yelling at the top of their lungs and pulling emergency buttons. The plane came to a screeching halt at the end of the runway.

God knows what might have happened had we actually taken off. We taxied back to the terminal, where we were served lunch — in a 100-degree cabin and amongst a chorus of bitching and complaining by the players. Finally, two hours later, after they'd thoroughly checked the plane out, we were ordered to deplane. Another jet was readied to take us to Utah.

Finally, some eight hours late, we took off at 4:00 P.M. Boston time. Everyone was beat. We were irritable, tired, and generally pissed off, particularly when we realized that the Broncos had merely had to make a forty-minute hop over the Rockies and had long since arrived in Salt Lake City.

By the time we arrived our buses had departed and we had to wait for new ones to be reordered. By the time they arrived it was fully thirteen and a half hours after we'd boarded the first plane and we were immediately dispatched to the stadium for a workout. On arriving we found that the gates were locked and had to wait around for a janitor to let us in. Around 10:00 P.M. Boston time we suited up for a light workout.

When, dead tired, we were at last taken to our hotel, I was greeted by a couple of my old Denver buddies, both of whom were absolutely polluted. "What took you so long," they slurred. The Broncos had worked out in Denver, jumped on the plane, and the guys were in the process of hitting all the hot spots in Salt Lake City. I was too tired to even undress. I passed out, fully clothed, from sheer exhaustion.

*

To top it all off both teams appeared for pregame warm-ups the next evening wearing the same color jerseys. The coaches, equipment managers, and players went wild, and after everyone tried to blame someone else, we set about trying to rectify the situation.

Finally the Broncos agreed to wear the University of Utah's uniforms. Both teams, naturally, played terrible football, and the long weekend was brought to a fitting climax when we were beaten in the last thirty seconds on a fifty-five-yard field goal — by none other than Bobby Howfield.

When it rains, it pours. And we still had that four-and-a-half-hour plane ride back. We arrived at Logan Airport at 7:00 in the morning. The Broncos made last call in Denver.

*

At least the rotten exhibition season was over. We were scheduled to open the season against the Miami Dolphins, who were by now coached by a guy named Don Shula. We still lacked a permanent home field and had to play at antiquated Harvard Stadium this year. Inasmuch as the locker rooms at Harvard were the size of a closet, we were dressing at the Ramada Inn in nearby Allston.

Just before the game, two of our starters, John Charles and Larry Carwell, both of whom were still unsigned, were on the trainer's table getting taped for the game when Clive Rush entered the room and demanded to know if the two planned on signing their contracts that day. Charles and Carwell repeated their desire to be paid more money before they'd sign.

In a low, nearly inaudible voice Rush told them to undress, that they were being deactivated from the roster. The rest of the team went into a state of shock. Here we were, playing one of the better teams in our division, and the coach was cutting two regular defensive backs an hour before kick-off.

One of our taxi squadders, former Notre Dame star Bob "Harpo" Gladieux, had awakened around 11:00 and decided he'd go to the game. Harpo had been cut earlier in the week, and in his own inimitable style had celebrated by, he recalls, "two solid days of ballin', drinkin', and carousin'." By Sunday morning, totally strung out, he'd showed up at Harvard Stadium with a friend.

Gladieux, though, didn't have a ticket for the game, and after several minutes of trying unsuccessfully to persuade the gate attendant that he was a member of the Patriots taxi squad, he bought a program. Turning to his picture, he showed the usher, who was still not entirely convinced. At last the guy let him in. Hung over, a bottle of wine in his pocket, he staggered up the stairs to the top of the stadium with his buddy to be far from the madding crowd in his misery.

Another taxi squad player, John Outlaw, had been summoned from his Dorchester apartment to fill one of the newly created roster vacancies. He was instructed to report to our training field at Curry College in Milton, dress in his uniform, and come to the game posthaste. Everything went according to plan until he got to the stadium. He filed through the crowd, the target of all sorts of weird looks and catcalls. The Pats had a reputation for being cheap, but this was ridiculous.

Then he approached the gate manned by the same attendant Harpo had just cajoled into letting him through. *"Oh, no!"* shouted the attendant. *"Enough's enough!"* First a guy who claims to be on the taxi squad and now some clown trying to crash the gate by wearing a uniform . . .

•

About twenty minutes before kick-off, Gladieux's friend had gone off in search of a couple of beers. Harpo was quietly sipping his wine when he heard an announcement over the public address system. *"Will Bob Gladieux please report to the Patriot locker room?"*

Harpo was in a state of panic. Clearly he was in no condition to play football under the circumstances. He was in a quandary, trying to make up his mind. Then he noticed the assistant coaches that work the press box during games were inadvertently approaching his seat. He hit the deck and tried to hide under the bleacher seat.

There, among 40,000 people, in the prone position, concealed from the naked eye, he made his decision to report. Knute Rockne would have been proud.

In the locker room, Clive Rush told him, "Suit up, Bob, you're playing in ten minutes." Defensive line coach Jesse

Richardson took one look at him and his face blanched. "Harpo, are you O.K.?"

"I think so," replied Harpo.

*

Meanwhile, Gladieux's friend had returned with the beers only to find Harpo gone. He was still scanning the stands in search of him when the game got underway. When after the opening kick-off the PA announced, "Tackle by Bob Gladieux," the guy fell right out of his seat. He knew he had the D.T.s for sure.

Despite all the pregame insanity and the bizarre last-minute changes, we went on to win that day. A professional athlete, they say, is paid to perform under conditions of adversity. That being the case, on that September 20 we earned every penny of our paychecks.

*

We reverted to form the following weekend and lost to the New York Jets. Then, the next Tuesday morning as I drove to practice, I sensed something eerie. There were a few score cars parked in front of the coaches' office at Curry College. There was a constant stream in and out of people carrying microphones, cameras, and tape recorders. I couldn't imagine what was happening. We were 1-1 and hadn't played that badly, so I knew Rush's job wasn't in jeopardy. Nance had signed several weeks earlier, so he wasn't the focus of all the commotion. Nobody in the locker room knew what was happening either.

After putting on my sweats, I joined the rest of the

players for the usual 12:00 meeting. After a few minutes Clive Rush entered the room, basking in a quixotic grin. "Gentlemen," he said, "I want to introduce our newest player, Joe Kapp."

There he was. I couldn't believe my eyes. The most colorful cat in the NFL, Joe Kapp. Eight months earlier I'd watched him on television directing the Minnesota Vikings against the Chiefs in the Super Bowl. Now he was my team-mate. "The living legend from the North Country," I was thinking. Now he'd be leading our team.

Mike Taliaferro, who'd been our starting quarterback, was shellshocked. He had as good an arm as anybody in football and had thrown seventeen touchdown passes the year before while ranking among the statistical leaders in the NFL. In fact, Mike had gotten off to a pretty fair start in 1970, but now Joe Kapp would be the whole show, the savior of the franchise.

Kapp was beautiful. Mentally, at least, he was ready to play. He had been suddenly and unexpectedly signed by the Patriots after playing out his option with Minnesota and had been widely reported to be the object of a blacklist all around the NFL. Perhaps Billy Sullivan had visions of championship trophies lining the corridors of Curry College, but whatever the case he signed Joe, blacklist or no black-list.

Joe Kapp was everything that's ever been written about him: machismo, charisma, you name it. He was brash and cocky, but he exuded confidence of the variety that is easily contagious. At the press conference held to announce his signing he was already talking seriously about titles for the

Boston Patriots. The guys took to Kapp like nails to a magnet, and Mike Taliaferro was quickly shoved into the background.

We were still tied for first place going into our third game, against the Baltimore Colts. Clive went with Taliaferro for the entire game, and the crowd was unmerciful. Cheering his every blunder, booing his every move, the chant of "We want Kapp" never let up throughout the game. At one point Mike faded back to pass and was buried beneath a whole host of Baltimore pass rushers. The fans cheered like hell. He was obviously shaken, and the Boston fans were rewarded: we lost.

❋

The next game was a sportswriter's dream. We were up against the Chiefs, and the game was immediately billed as "Kapp's Revenge." He would take command of his troops and lead them into battle with his erstwhile conquerors from Kansas City.

It had taken Kapp just five days to pass Kim Hammond and move up to number two on the depth chart, but Taliaferro was still down to start the game. Beyond that, the line-up changes were mind-boggling.

During practice that week Rush had devised an intricate scheme calculated to totally confuse the world champs. It confused us even more. He switched the offensive line around completely. Most of the guys on the line had played together for the past several years, but all of a sudden Rush moved All-Pro center Jon Morris to offensive guard, switched guard Mike Montler to tackle, and brought rookie defensive end Denny Wirgowski over to handle Morris' position. Starting offensive tackle Tom Funchess was switched to Wirgowski's vacated spot, and finally, Len St. Jean moved from left to right guard.

Needless to say, it was a very chaotic week in practice. Offensive drills were continually screwed up as people jumped offside, blocked the wrong man, pulled the wrong way, and generally botched assignments. I spent the week in utter amazement. Experimenting with a new line-up against the Super Bowl champs. No way!

＊

We flew to Kansas City and practiced at a small field adjacent to Municipal Stadium. No sooner had the offensive unit lined up to run dummy scrimmages than Coach Rush instructed all the players he'd switched earlier in the week to return to their original positions. Everyone sort of looked at one another and, moving like robots, switched back again. Nobody said a word, but everyone was thinking, "What the hell is with this guy, anyway?"

On October 11, 1970, the Kansas City Chiefs had little trouble pummeling us, 23-10. I'm sure it didn't hurt their cause at all that half of our line didn't know their game assignments.

It was actually more of a rout than the score would indicate. For me, it was the fourth time I'd played in Kansas City, and since I'd just lost there for the fourth straight time I felt right at home. Joe Kapp did play some but could do little more than run out of fear for his life. While he'd done his best without success to rally us, it had proven to be his baptism of fire in the red, white, and blue of Boston.

At least there were only ten games to go.

❃

The New York Giants are the Patriots' archrivals. The Giants had been in pro football a lot longer than us, of course, but there was also the fact that their games were being telecast all over New England long before the Pats existed — and continued to be long after the Patriots entered the scene. As a result, they continued to have as many fans in the area as we did. Ergo, the rivalry was a natural. For the fans, for the owners of the two clubs, and for television, that is. The sportswriters had to tell the players that we weren't supposed to like each other because, after all, we were competing for the same share of the market — in this case all those enthusiastic football fans in Hartford and Providence. This, then, was Giant Week, and the New Yorkers were coming to town to play us at Harvard Stadium in the first match-up in history between the two teams.

The local media outdid themselves shilling for the game. For the first time in years the Patriots had a sellout at home. In large measure we hadn't had one in years because the local fans preferred to watch the Giants on TV than the Patriots live.

Kapp was going to start at quarterback. It had taken him two weeks of practice to displace Taliaferro, although the vicious attitude of the fans toward Mike certainly hadn't helped him in management's eyes. From the moment the Patriots had acquired Kapp, Taliaferro had been a fallen gladiator and the people in the stands had held their thumbs toward hell, a disgraceful performance for what is supposed to be the best sports town in the country. They had, though, gotten their wish, and Taliaferro was eased out in Kapp's favor.

Ah, and it was a fine day for Billy Sullivan as well. In the program that Sunday there was a flowery letter from Sullivan, smelling of roses and daffodils. It was an embarrassing paean to Giants owner Wellington Mara, so chock filled with thank you's that I was thoroughly embarrassed as I read it in the locker room. I looked up and saw that linebacker Fred Whittingham and Bob Gladieux were also reading it. Harpo shook his head and belched. Whittingham laughed.

Physically and mentally we should have been ready for the Giants; we'd been keying ourselves up all week. But from the moment we stepped out onto the field I felt my heart sink. We were in trouble, perhaps big trouble. The wind had picked up during the morning and was already blowing up a storm. Kapp was never noted for his pinpoint passing in the first place; in a twenty-five-mph wind he'd be next to useless.

My powers of deduction were impeccable. The game was nothing short of a disaster. We might have been able to handle the Giants, but trying to contend with the weather was another thing entirely. Poor Joe couldn't begin to control his passes. Everything he put in the air looked like Hoyt Wilhelm pitching in a wind tunnel. We were shut out for the first time in years. Apparently Sullivan's ode to the Maras didn't inspire any mercy on the part of the Giants.

We had lost the game, the symbolic "New England Su-

premacy," and of course the potential loyalty of those bor-
derline Giant fans who might have been teetering on the
brink of defection. I also noticed that on occasion boos and
sneers from the stands were directed toward Kapp. Not
even Joe could avoid the wrath of the Boston fans.

＊

A week later we journeyed to Baltimore, having run our losing streak to four games already. On the plane we were each
personally handed a brown paper bag by general manager
George Sauer. The contents: two sandwiches, an apple, and
a slice of pound cake. "How bush can you get?" trainer Bill
Bates demanded irately. "At least the pound cake could
have had some icing." I knew the Patriots were cheap, but
this was ridiculous.

Coach Rush missed the bus to practice in Baltimore. We
should have missed the plane in Boston. The Colts tore us
apart 27-3 for our fifth loss in a row.

Life as a Patriot was becoming morbid. We were already
deeply buried in the cellar of our division. Sometimes I
thought back to the Bronco days, but it wasn't really the
same thing at all. In Denver we'd had a young team, twenty
rookies at one time during the year. Inexperience accounted
for our ineptitude.

Boston didn't. The Patriots had a lot of veteran players,
while only four rookies had made the team. The franchise,
very simply, was in deep trouble. All of a sudden all the
years of misadministration, rotten drafts, stupid trades, and
aging players had come to a head and they were taking a toll.
In Denver we could at least kid ourselves by looking to the

future. In Boston the practice was to look back at the past and reminisce about the golden years under Mike Holovak, the days of Babe Parilli. I took my rosary out of mothballs. I figured we needed help from upstairs.

❋

Clive Rush was acting stranger and stranger. What had passed for eccentricity before began to appear more serious. During the week he was rarely on the field for practice and seldom in the meeting rooms. He had become visibly distraught, wrung-out, and tired. Offensive coordinator John Mazur ran the show for the offense, while his defensive counterpart, Bill Elias, handled his end. Clive had become a phantom coach, and rumors bounced all over the locker room. The Buffalo Bills team we were facing that week had nearly as many problems as we did. They were wallowing in mediocrity, had twelve rookies on their roster, and some players were openly criticizing the coaching staff.

❋

During pregame warm-ups one of the team physicians, Dr. Burton Nault, checked Coach Rush's pulse and ordered him back to the hotel to rest. It was apparent that the multitude of pressures inflicted on Clive by the media and the fans — and our obsessive proclivity for losing football games — had finally taken their toll. He had broken down.

As individuals and as a team we knew what Clive was going through. It was pure hell. Less than two years before the man had coached an offense that had brought the first Super Bowl championship to an AFL team. He had been the architect of the game plan by which Joe Namath had riddled the fabled Baltimore zone defense, and now he was saddled with a collection of turkeys who didn't know how to do anything but lose. Not even the presence of Joe Kapp had been able to improve our performance.

With Mazur hurriedly taking over the team, we were humiliated by the equally inept Bills that afternoon by a score of 45 to 10. A line of police had to be formed to cordon off our bench. The crowd was pretty ugly, pelting us with food, paper cups, and assorted debris. No doubt they would have formed a lynch mob and attacked us had the police not been there for protection.

Clive Rush returned to the field at half time and tried to rally us, but if anything his exhortations had a negative effect. We just felt sorry for him. It was clear that our entire organizational structure was in shreds and on the brink of total collapse, and we just went through the motions. To a man we realized that at that moment we were by far the worst team in professional football.

Meanwhile, the fans almost tore Rush apart. They were shouting the most horrendous insults imaginable. He was already done, yet the "greatest sports fans in the country" were determined to put one more nail in his coffin. They succeeded.

*

That night a diehard Patriot booster named Sid Cohen tossed a party for the team at his Newton home. A number of the players gathered in small clusters and whispered in contemplation of the immediate future. We had a six-game losing streak, an ailing coach, and seven games left to play. Some of the former players who'd retired over the past few years, like Bob Dee and Larry Eisenhauer, were present and joined in the conversations, but while we searched for answers until the wee hours of the morning, none were forthcoming.

As I pulled up in the driveway for practice Tuesday, prepared to watch our embarrassment recorded on film, I noticed the fleet of cars assembled in front of the coaches' office immediately. Something, obviously, was happening.

Something did happen. Billy Sullivan had relieved Clive Rush "for medical reasons" and installed John Mazur as interim head coach. Now the Patriots had three head coaches on the payroll: Holovak, Rush, and Mazur. Clive refused at first to step down; he had already spurned Sullivan's request that he announce he was leaving voluntarily, and he angrily told the press that the "medical reasons" story was a sham, that there was nothing wrong with him, and that he was being eased out.

You couldn't blame the guy. It was the same old story — he hadn't lost the games, we had. He was a proven winner.

*

Mazur locked the doors for the team meeting, coaches and players only. What had happened in the past, he told us, would be forgotten. From now on in he would work us until we'd done our jobs correctly. No more one-hour practices; we would have three meetings a day from now on. He was, in brief, trying to initiate at once some badly needed discipline.

Some players balked right away at the new regimen. "What's the difference?" they were asking. "We're not challenging for any goddamn championship." They reasoned that there seemed to be little reason to suddenly start busting their asses when we were 1-6. I believe the disease is called dissension.

Practices became more serious, a lot tougher, and a lot longer. Mazur meant business. The laughter, joking, and general screwing off ceased and bungholes started to quiver again. We even ran sprints after practice, something unheard of on the Patriots, but due to our generally poor physical condition, quite necessary.

Unfortunately, our renewed vigor didn't make us as good as the St. Louis Cardinals. They were leading the tough Eastern Division of the NFC, and we were hopelessly outclassed, 31-0. We had tried, but when one sportswriter described us as "pitiful, at best," for once he wasn't twisting the facts. We were indeed pitiful.

As hard as we were working during the week, the talent on our ball club simply didn't measure up to the rest of the league. While we had good young players like Carl Garrett and Ron Sellers and proven veterans like Nance and Kapp, the overall personnel scarcely posed an intimidating threat to anybody.

And that old bugaboo, injuries, also began to make itself felt. At one point our entire offensive line resembled the walking wounded at Valley Forge. The ones who weren't in the hospital already, that is. Kapp had begun to sense that his new team bore little resemblance to his old Vikings. People like Gary Bugenhagen, Ezell Jones, and Angelo Loukas were hardly capable of shutting the gates, and Kapp, who had started running for his life in the fourth quarter of the Chiefs game, never did stop running. By our ninth consecutive loss his entire body looked like chopped liver.

✻

We flew to Buffalo for a return match with the Bills. They hadn't won either, since the 45-10 game. On Saturday night most of the veterans congregated at a suburban lounge named Sestak–Maguire's, partly owned by Buffalo punter Paul Maguire. He was always good for the latest scuttlebutt about the Bills, and we countered with our own woes. After several hours of comparing franchises, we all concluded that we were both in deep trouble.

Harpo Gladieux started to relate his experiences during his brief career with the Bills. He'd been placed on waivers earlier in the year and picked up by Buffalo. An assistant coach had left instructions to meet him in the lobby of a Buffalo hotel the following day. Harpo had showed up wearing tie-dyed jeans, a matching tie-dyed shirt, boots, sunglasses, and a fringed leather jacket. Along with his long curly hair and mustache, it all made him look like part of a rock group.

The coach was already waiting when Harpo arrived but didn't say anything to his new acquisition.

Harpo waited. The coach waited. Occasionally the coach would leer at Gladieux venomously as he muttered to himself.

Finally, after forty-five minutes of waiting, Harpo approached the Ivy-League-attired Bills' aide and asked, "Are you waiting for Bob Gladieux?"

The coach stared at him. "Oh, my God!"

The Bills weren't ready for Harpo. His first official practice was disastrous — he got lost on the turnpike and missed half the workout. Then, that Sunday, he played in the game and sparkled on special teams. Two days later, before the Tuesday meeting, Buffalo head man John Rauch summoned him to his office.

"We haven't made many mistakes since I've come to Buffalo," said Rauch, "but bringing you here was one."

It all worked out in the end. He was reclaimed by the Patriots, the team that had cut him ten days earlier. You figure that one out.

*

We played well in Buffalo, and believe it or not, Mr. Ripley, we won the battle of the have-nots, 14-10. Then there was more action outside the stadium after the game.

We were walking to the buses when gunshots rang out. Some guys immediately hit the deck, others ran for the buses. It seems that down the street the police were shooting it out with the occupants of an old, dilapidated house.

In a true gesture of flower power, Gladieux wanted to walk down the street waving a white handkerchief. We managed to dissuade him. The whole episode was not at all incongruous with Buffalo; War Memorial Stadium was located in the worst section of the city, and it was considered dangerous to walk to a game. The vice president of the Bills was once mugged after a game, as was Bill kicker Booth Lustig, but still, I don't think any other team in the NFL could have wound up in the middle of a gunfight.

*

We needed the modicum of confidence the Buffalo victory inspired. The next opponent was Miami, a young, hungry team we'd beaten earlier in the year. They were in a dogfight for first place in the division.

It was seemingly over within a matter of minutes. Mercury Morris ran the opening kick-off right through the middle of our coverage, going ninety-six yards to score. Then we moved the ball to the Miami forty-two, but when Gino Cappelletti tried a field goal it was blocked by Manny Fernandez. Lloyd Mumphord picked up the ball and scampered fifty-one yards to score again. There were fifty-six minutes to play, the Miami offense hadn't set foot on the field, and here we were behind, 14-0. Their fans were already waving white handkerchiefs.

For once we did valiantly try to fight back, and at one point in the second quarter we had actually closed the gap to 17-7. Kapp, though, was under constant pressure from the Dolphins' front four, and on one play he tried to scramble and was hit by three guys at once. He got up, wobbly on his feet, but from then on he was calling plays in the huddle that nobody else had ever heard of.

Our makeshift offensive line was like a sieve. On one play, reserve guard Gary Bugenhagen pulled for a sweep. In the process he (a) stepped on Tom Funchess' foot and (b) subsequently fell on Montler's leg, forcing both of them out of the game. During the time out Kapp walked over to the bench and demanded that Mazur take Bugenhagen out of the game before he wiped out what was left of the line.

The Dolphins rolled, 37-20. On the plane back to Boston I didn't hear a word about football, although we had two games left. Everybody was talking about Christmas and travel and skiing and off-season jobs, but with the Minnesota Vikings coming up the next week nobody seemed to care about football. All anyone really cared about was landing early enough to hit a few bars before last call.

*

All week long Kapp tried to inspire us, the offensive line in particular. Not only would we establish the worst record in team history by losing, but Joe wanted badly to beat his old teammates. He was also more than a little concerned about being devoured by the Purple People Eaters. He must have felt like a guy going to the chair trying to beg his way to an eleventh-hour reprieve from the governor.

*

The night before the game it began snowing. Snow fell throughout the night and into the early afternoon, and by game time Harvard Stadium was covered. The Patriot management hadn't touched the place, and each and every seat was buried under a nine-inch heap of snow. Our bench was one gigantic snowdrift.

The fans were understandably irate. They'd paid, after all, $7.50 apiece to sit in a snowbank. The temperature hovered in the midteens, and when we took the field we were greeted with a barrage of snowballs. Some of our guys fell down immediately; it was like running barefoot on ice. We tried to run pass patterns and couldn't. We couldn't even stand up.

By contrast, the Vikings sprinted out wearing special

sneakers constructed specifically for playing on frozen surfaces. They had come 1500 miles and they were better equipped and prepared than we were, the home team.

Some of our players began to panic. Punter Tom Janik, who was destined for a long afternoon, used a pair of ripple-soled shoes belonging to one of the coaches. A few key players — Garrett, Nance, Sellers, and a couple of defensive backs — followed suit and traded shoes with the coaches. The balance of the squad had to do the best they could. The first time the Vikings had the ball they scored. Flanker John Henderson sprinted by a helpless Daryl Johnson, who looked like he was treading water. Bob Lee arched a lazy pass to Henderson, who never broke stride all the way to the end zone.

By half time the scoreboard read 21 to 7. Our equipment manager George Luongo had brought in forty pairs of sneakers from a nearby sporting goods store, but by then, of course, it was too late. Fourteen points might as well be a million against a defense like Minnesota's. The Vikes completely dominated the game, outgaining us by a ratio of nearly four to one. Alan Page and Carl Eller rushed at will and spent more time in our backfield than our backs did. Kapp, meanwhile, was a victim of brutal bodily assault at the hands of his one-time compadres. Still, he kept coming back for more; I've never met a guy with more desire and tenacity.

While the Vikings were playing beanbag with Kapp, the remaining fans were up to their old tricks. We were pelted by a constant hail of snowballs, ice balls, and worst of all, rock balls. Some geniuses up in the upper stands were stuffing stones into medium-sized snowballs and hurling them from the top of the stadium. The cops instructed us to keep our helmets on at all times. Some of the players started tossing the missiles back. Can you imagine that — people had paid $7.50 a whack to come have a snowball fight with the Boston Patriots?

After the game an old buddy of mine, John Beasley, the Vikings tight end, asked me in amazement, "How could you guys expect to win if you couldn't even stand up out there?" I couldn't give him an answer. All I said was "The game was a near sellout. That's what's important to the team's owners." "Who the hell cares if we win or lose," I was thinking, "just as long as the park is filled on Sunday and you can write letters extolling the virtues of Wellington Mara for the program."

I had to excuse myself and barf.

*

We had one more game to go, and morale was lower than the River Styx. Everybody just wanted to get it over with and go home. We were facing the Cincinnati Bengals, who had to win to gain a play-off spot in the AFC. To us, it meant one more paycheck. The newspapers gleefully pointed out that, being the Patriots, we would probably screw up and win, costing us our locked-up number one draft choice.

The locker room at Riverfront Stadium in Cincinnati looked like a hardware store. Many players were going home right after the ball game, and they had brought along television sets, stereos, radios, luggage, furniture, and clothes bags. Somebody even brought a rifle. Before the game guys were sitting around discussing travel plans, best routes, alternate routes, airplane reservations, and connections. Instead of playbooks the Patriots were studying road maps and airline timetables.

Not surprisingly, the Bengals pushed us all over the field. From the opening kick-off they beat the holy hell out of us. As bad as we'd played all year, we'd never come close to being this horrendous. The Bengals scored every single time they had the ball in the first half; by the time the band marched out at the midway point it was already 38 to 0.

Coach Mazur was livid. He called our performance, quite correctly, putrid. I had visions of an 80-0 or 90-0 game. It was embarrassing.

Paul Brown undoubtedly told his charges to hold it down, and midway through the third quarter we actually made our first first down. The final score was 45-7, but at least our unforgettable 1970 season had come to an end.

Players quickly dressed and split, road maps and plane tickets in hand. I flew back to Boston, thinking of a long, quiet off season in Houston and reflecting on the past five months. I'd seen an entire team disintegrate before my eyes, and yes, I'd been part of it. When you've played for a 2-12 season there's plenty of soul-searching to do. I was just thankful it was over and I still was in one piece!

7

Those Thrilling Days of Yesteryear

SHOOTING THE SHIT about bygone days is a characteristic of any occupation in which people work together for any length of time, and football teams are certainly no exception. I discovered almost immediately, though, that the Patriots' history offered more than its share of material for barroom bull sessions. As the year progressed I found that the older veterans like Len St. Jean, Jon Morris, and Gino Cappelletti could always be counted on to come up with a blast from the past. Sometimes their recollections would leave listeners open-mouthed and incredulous, and on other occasions they were capable of sending an entire table full of players rolling on the floor in laughter.

Trainer Bill Bates had been an original member of the organization. A couple of years later Bates himself would be the fall guy in an episode not at all atypical in the annals of the Patriots. After the 1971 season, when Upton Bell failed in his bid to dismiss coach John Mazur, he retaliated by inexplicably firing Bates, public relations director Jack Nicholson, Nicholson's assistant Wally Carew, and a secretary

in the front office. Since Bates was widely regarded as one
of the best trainers in professional sports (he immediately
got a job with the Milwaukee Bucks and says that he now
sends Upton a Christmas card each year thanking him for the
blessing in disguise), the consensus of opinion held that Bell
was acting out of spite. *"See here, Board of Directors. If I
can't fire the coach I still have enough power to fire the
trainer and the PR man. So there!"*

Bates's initial clue of things to come occurred on the Patriots' first road game. "We had a charter flight to Denver,
where we were playing the Broncos. I think this was early
nineteen sixty, and we'd left Boston about noon. An hour or
so later I was looking out the window and getting more and
more curious. Now, I'm not Leif Ericson or Charles Lind-
bergh, but we seemed to be flying due north. For a game in
Denver? I didn't know whether we were taking the Arctic
route or what.

"Anyway, after an hour or so we landed. In Buffalo.
Then the Buffalo Bills started filing on. It seems that, with-
out telling anyone, the teams had decided to share a plane.
The Bills were playing on the Coast that weekend," laughed
Bates.

"So both teams flew to Denver, where they dropped us off.
Trouble was, there was no ramp waiting for us in Denver.
The airline improvised. They drove a food truck right up
beside the plane, and we deplaned that way, jumping out on
top of the food truck and then descending via stepladder
from the cab of the truck." This was pro football?

❖

Buffalo stories were always popular. During the exhibition season the team would fly into Buffalo on the day of the game in order to skimp on expenses. If that wasn't bad enough, instead of the standard fifty dollars in expense money, players were provided with forty-five dollars. They were instructed not to lie down in the beds, break the seal on the toilets, or use the towels in the hotel rooms; if they complied they'd get the extra five bucks.

Larry Eisenhauer, one of the original wild men on the early Patriots, went on a search-and-destroy mission through the hotel, going from room to room tearing beds apart. Considering what salaries were back in the early days of the AFL, it was a pretty expensive practical joke for some struggling players.

The following year, again during the exhibition season, the Patriots went a step further. Apparently incensed over the hotel episode of the previous season, this time the management arrived at the hotel on the day of the game and herded the team into a general meeting room called the Niagara or the Mohawk or some damned thing. Six hours before game time, and the players had three options: sit on a chair, lie on the floor, or if you were lucky, lie on a table. It was a great way to prepare for a football game.

*

Mike Holovak was one of the early Patriot head coaches. During the Holovak era, Billy Sullivan's son Patrick worked as a ball boy and doubled as Holovak's "Turk":

"I was all of twelve years old, and he used to make me cut players. He'd send me to a player's room. I'd have to knock

on the door and say, 'The coach wants to see you. Bring
your playbook.' It was terrible. It got so that everyone
hated the sight of me. If they saw me coming they'd curse,
throw helmets at me. To this day I can tell guys who were
around then like Morris and St. Jean still get uneasy when
they see me."

Holovak also harbored an abhorrence for arriving early
for a contest. The team would invariably arrive just before
game time. Once the Patriots were playing the Houston Oilers in Rice Stadium and, after leaving the hotel just an hour
before the scheduled kick-off, got stuck in a traffic jam en
route to the stadium. Arriving barely fifteen minutes before
the game, the bus driver let the panicking Patriots out in a
nearby parking lot. The team had to run through the stands,
carrying suitcases and equipment bags.

One lady stopped Gino Cappelletti and asked him if this
was indeed the opposing team. "No, Ma'am," replied the
Duke. "We're the half-time entertainment."

Another time the Patriots were playing the Chargers in
San Diego and had to catch a flight back to Boston shortly
after the game. As the game rolled on, it became apparent
that the Pats were in a race against time to catch the plane.
Although the team was getting massacred on the field, the
coaching staff was more obsessed with getting to the airport
on time and the equipment was being packed up well before
the game was over. Players were instructed to get dressed
as quickly as possible, and some guys didn't even have time
to take showers. The entourage then sped for the airport, just making it on time.

When the team reported for the Tuesday meeting everyone was worried. They'd played miserably against the Chargers, and many asses were due to be severely chewed. Instead Holovak congratulated the team on getting to the plane on time.

Another time the team was playing an exhibition game in Norfolk, Virginia. The flight was delayed, and since the Patriots were naturally flying in on the day of the game, the trainers had to break out their equipment and start taping ankles in flight. After landing, the equipment bags were distributed on the buses and fifty-some-odd players had to don their pads and uniforms in transit to the stadium.

Holovak's Patriots trained during the summer at Phillips Academy in Andover. Presumably the team was housed according to the amount of money the Pats management was willing to spend, because they were housed in an antediluvian dormitory. In lieu of fire escapes, each floor on the upper stories was provided with a knotted rope that you were supposed to climb down in case of emergency. There were a number of nonfootball-related injuries during the Andover days, as not a few players fell several stories from the ropes. And of course the heavier players had to forego ducking out after curfew altogether. Those knotted ropes weren't made to hold a 280-pound tackle.

The regular season training site was a dingy high school stadium in East Boston. The facilities were ludicrous: tiny locker rooms furnished with milk cartons to sit on. The trainer's room was located in a closet, and the game films were shown on a torn sheet nailed to the wall. The Decatur Staleys and the Canton Bulldogs, I am sure, had better facilities fifty years ago. The East Boston field did have one ad-

vantage though: it was located ten minutes away from
Suffolk Downs.

•

One year Bill Bates returned early to East Boston to clean up
his equipment for the upcoming season only to find everything missing. After a frantic search and a call to report a
theft, someone finally came up with the information that
everything had been carted off to Cape Cod. Former baseball great Don DiMaggio, then one of the owners, had volunteered his garage as a storage site, although naturally no
one had bothered to notify Bates.

The Patriots' scouting in the early days was handled by
Holovak and general manager Ed McKeever. In order to cut
down on expenses, the team frequently "scouted" a player
by sending him a questionnaire printed on the back of a pre-
paid post card. The prospect would fill in the pertinent information, vital statistics, etc., and return it to the team,
which would place it on file.

There was also an unwritten rule employed by the Patriot
management when it came to the annual college draft. The
team seldom drafted a player from west of the Mississippi.
The logic was exquisitely simple: why spend money on the
additional airfare when you could draft a guy you could
bring in for subway fare. Western and midwestern players
were shunned. McKeever, from Louisiana, selected a number of players from the south. Holovak, from Massachusetts,
favored players from the east, and there was a resultant pot-
pourri of Yankees and Rebels. With both Holovak and Sullivan having Boston College connections, a number of home-

town boys also found favor with the Patriots; at one time there were no less than eight B.C. alumni on the roster, as well as two more players — Bob Dee and Jon Morris — from Holy Cross.

The Patriots also wasted a lot of draft choices. Number one picks such as Tulane's Tommy Mason, B.C.'s Jack Concannon, Maryland's Gary Collins, and Alabama's Lee Roy Jordan never donned a Boston uniform. They all signed with the NFL. On the other hand, other high draft picks — Karl Singer, Gerhard Schwedes, Dennis Byrd, Jim Boudreaux, Rick Arrington, et al. — signed but could not play football very well.

While the reliance on local talent worked for a while — in the early AFL years, the Pats teams comprised of the B.C., B.U., Holy Cross, and Harvard grads combined with McKeever's southerners had fared well — it would hardly keep apace with the growth of the rest of the league. The combination of poor overall drafting, lack of foresight, and antiquated methods eventually caught up with the Patriots, with disastrous results. The team hasn't had a winning season since 1966.

In the late 1960s, recalls Bill Bates, the Patriots coveted a particular player from the south. He'd starred in a bowl game and been named to some All-American teams the preceding year, and the team was all set to draft him. Moments before they announced their selection, someone notified the Patriots that their prospect had been killed in an automobile accident nearly a year before.

*

My first official publicity shot as a Bronco. One thing about Colorado, you never have to worry about running out of fertilizer.

A typical Bronco pass — 5 yards over my head!

It wasn't uncommon for players to catch
40 winks during a Clive Rush practice.
Too bad we played the same way Sunday.
Pamela R. Schuyler

Stretching for glory. A typical Patriots training session at the University of Massachusetts, Amherst. *Pamela R. Schuyler*

Upton Bell, the dynamic force behind the "Patriots Revolution." His poker struggles with Billy Sullivan ultimately led to his demise. *Michael Dobo*

When John Mazur took the team to camp in 1971, he brought back the infamous "meat grinder" and other agonizing drills. The party was over. *Pamela R. Schuyler*

Linebacker Steve Kiner was acclaimed as the Patriots'
best defensive player in 1971. The next year he was traded
for a marginal third-stringer. Figure it out! *Ed Moore*

Right: Jim Plunkett brought a hope for the future to the
Patriots. He paid for his popularity. *Pamela R. Schuyler*

Indeed 1972 was a nightmare. This scene was typical of a
perfectly thrown Plunkett pass. *Kevin Galvin/Photo-Sport*

Phil Bengtson — author of the top-secret, mysterious "Bengtson Report." *Michael Dobo*

Here's a pair that would beat a full house any day of the week — the inimitable Howard Cosell and Patriots owner Billy Sullivan. *Jeff Adler*

Patriots head coach Chuck Fairbanks: "One picture is worth a thousand words."

Six months after Fairbanks took over as coach of the Patriots, this is all that was left from the John Mazur era. Rest in peace.

During the 1973 season Buffalo's O. J. Simpson rushed for over 500 yards against the porous Patriots defense. Back to the drawing board. *Kevin Galvin/Photo-Sport*

Jim Plunkett — the ray of hope for the foundering New England franchise.

Waning moments — as a Miami Dolphin.

Bob Schmertz, owner of the WFL New York Stars, proudly displays the contract of former New York Jet John Elliott. Elliott was the first of many legitimate NFL stars to jump leagues. *Lee Rosner*

When Holovak was finally eased out of the picture, the Patriots turned to the genius behind the New York Jets offense, Clive Rush. Unlike Holovak, Rush was an excitable sort who frequently made spur-of-the-moment, impulsive decisions. His career with the Patriots was brief, but it was very nearly briefer. At his first press conference as head coach, Rush touched a microphone and received a shock that jolted him right out of his chair. It was, in retrospect, an omen for the future.

Will McDonough, who covered the Patriots for the Boston *Globe* during the Rush era, remembers a time when the team was just about to depart for a game in New York. Everyone had boarded and was in his seat, when Rush suddenly ordered all the media people off the plane. The reporters reluctantly complied and stood at the bottom of the ramp waiting to find out what the hell was going on.

When the press returned to the plane, McDonough, baffled, asked one of the stewardesses what had transpired in his absence. "Oh, he told the players that Harvard would allow the team to play there next year," she replied.

McDonough, mildly stunned, shook his head. "Oh," he said to himself. "Of course."

Upon arriving in New York, the team was heading to Shea Stadium for practice when Rush suddenly halted the bus he was riding in. There was no music on the bus, and Clive wanted to hear some music. It turned out that one of the players on the second bus had a cassette player, which he loaned to the coach. Mollified, Rush then directed the driver to proceed, and the team zinged down the highway while Clive snapped his fingers to the beat.

Rush was a likable guy with an eminently sound football mind. The Patriots' whacky operation eventually got to him, though, and sent him to an early retirement.

On one occasion in 1969 the Pats were playing the Chargers on the Coast and after a few questionable calls, Clive stormed right out onto the field in a rage. The Chargers broke their huddle and when Lance Alworth went to line up in the slot, Clive was standing directly in his spot, still railing at the officials. The Pats were heavily penalized.

*

One time the Patriots had flown to Houston days before the game only to discover that the chartered buses were nowhere in sight. Rush, without batting an eye, ordered a whole fleet of cabs — eighteen or twenty of them — to ferry the players to the hotel, twenty-five miles away. The cost was undoubtedly astronomical, particularly for a team that scouted via post cards.

After the last cab had arrived at the Houston Marriott and the room keys had been distributed, Bill Bates was walking down the hall to his room when he passed Rush's. The door was open, and there in plain sight was general manager George Sauer trying to strangle PR man Jack Nicholson. Nicholson had arrived in Houston a few days early, as is standard practice in the NFL, to prep the local press on the Patriots and drum up interest for the game. Apparently he'd exhausted the funds the team had provided for his trip and had had the temerity to ask Sauer for more bread, prompting the general manager to throttle him. Rush managed to break up the skirmish just as Nicholson was turning purple, and the gagging PR man fled the premises.

The team worked out in Houston all week. One day Rush became annoyed by the roundabout route the bus was taking back to the hotel. He ordered the driver to stop, got out, and proceeded to halt all the traffic while directing the bus right to the door of a hotel — going the wrong way on a one-way street.

●

"It's funny," recalls Bill Bates, "but most of the memories that come to mind when I think about my days with the Patriots usually find the team screwing somebody. That's probably why they've been losers since the midsixties."

●

Could be. It's certainly happened enough. But for every story like Gino Cappelletti's — the Duke was abruptly axed by Mazur in a power move in his struggle with Bell, a cruel fate for an all-time AFL All-Star — there is another side. One night defensive coordinator Dick Evans was mangled by an attack dog at Schaefer Stadium. Once linebacker Don McKinnon broke the wedge on a kick-off only to have an instant attack of diarrhea. Frequently management may have been the villain in the tragicomedy that has been the history of the Patriots, but the other dramatis personae — the players themselves — have fit a Keystone Kops' role all too well.

There was a fellow named Chuck Close who hung around the team back in the sixties. He became very friendly with the players. A fanatical Patriot fan, Chuck Close, even made several road trips, a true show of allegiance. He was given various odd jobs and meaningless tasks by team officials, just because he so obviously wanted to be part of the Patriot family.

After several weeks Chuck Close began to borrow money. A ten here, a twenty there. He hit a few players for even more than that, but he hit *everybody*.

Then one day Chuck Close disappeared. He was nowhere to be found. As the weeks went by players began to get impatient, particularly the guys who'd been tapped heavily.

Eventually a couple of the guys went to the police to check the situation out. At the station the cops produced some mug shots of bunco artists, and there he was. Chuck Close was regarded as one of the best. I'm sure he's somewhere right now laughing about his days with the Patriots. After all, they say a sucker is born every minute.

But where else could you find forty of them on one football team?

8

A Pocketful of Miracles

By VIRTUE of having the worst record in the NFL in 1970 the
Patriots were privileged to select first in the college draft
that year. There was no inconsiderable degree of speculation that we might trade our number one pick for established players, and the scuttlebutt was not without foundation. Dallas and Baltimore, just to name two teams, were
willing to part with a veritable king's ransom in order to be
in a position to select a kid from Stanford named Jim Plunkett, who was everyone's choice to be the first selection. He'd
been an All-American on every team selected and barely a
month before had led Stanford to victory over Ohio State in
the Rose Bowl.

John Mazur had been retained as head coach, and he made
the decision to keep the draft choice and select Plunkett. It
marked the first time in years that the Patriots had drafted a
legitimate superstar. In years gone by the team's scouting
department had ranged from incompetent to nonexistent,
and it was rumored that the Patriots had actually based

their selections on the *Street & Smith College Football Magazine* one year.

＊

A few weeks before the draft I'd received a call from receiver coach Jerry Stoltz. "Bulk up, Tom," Stoltz had told me. "We're going to move you to offensive guard. We need somebody who can block there." I accepted the dictum, albeit reluctantly. Goodbye glory, hello pit. It would be a change, but I agreed and set about the task of putting on another thirty pounds of beef by hitting the weights.

Months later, after I'd bulked up to 250, the coaching staff decided it wanted me to play tight end after all. I just shrugged it off. I'd grown accustomed to this sort of thing by then. I was playing for the Patriots, wasn't I?

＊

In February Billy Sullivan had announced the signing of Upton Bell to the post of general manager. The son of NFL pioneer and Commissioner Bert Bell, Upton was young, handsome, and cocky; he was given "complete control" over the operations of the team. He had, after all, as player personnel director built the Baltimore Colts team that had just won the Super Bowl, and while he was brash and a showman, unlike other NFL showmen Bell knew football. He announced that he was going to perform another miracle with the Patriots, the laughingstock of the NFL.

Things seemed to have taken a turn for the better. The gloomy forecast that inevitably followed our dismal season began to evaporate with the advent of the Bell regime. We had Mazur back, of course, and we had Jim Plunkett. It was as if respectability had been visited on us overnight. And, best of all, we were finally going to have a stadium of our own. Schaefer Stadium in Foxboro, situated midway between Boston and Providence, was under construction and would be ready by the start of the exhibition season.

The old, tired image of the Boston Patriots would be buried forever. The board of directors initially renamed the team the "Bay State Patriots," but a few days of newspapermen making reference to the "B.S. Patriots" changed that. (The fact that B.S. also happened to be the initials of one Billy Sullivan, who resides on Bay State Road in suburban Wellesley, might have also had something to do with it.) The franchise eventually wound up being called the New England Patriots, presumably to give the team regional appeal. They'd have named us anything, as long as they could fill Schaefer Stadium on Sundays.

Bell didn't dawdle in asserting his presence. He hired faster than he fired. While he was cleaning house in the office, purging the legacy he had inherited, he was hiring the likes of Peter Hadhazy away from the NFL commissioner's office to serve as assistant general manager and Bucko Kilroy from the Dallas organization to revamp the Patriot's miserable scouting system as director of player personnel. He also engaged the services of the highly respected Herman Bruce to serve as business manager.

Our distraught fans began to forget about the holocausts of the past and looked ahead, with us, to the future. In the first few months they were available, season ticket sales doubled, while Bell, playing his role like a carnival barker, began to assemble a team around his two Chicano quarterbacks, Plunkett and Kapp.

A local radio talk show even got caught up in the excitement of Bell's revolution. "Sports Huddle," a successful program on WEEI in Boston, launched something called the "Search for Superfoot." Eddie Andelman, Mark Witkin, and Jim McCarthy, the show's hosts, flew to England where, in conjunction with cosponsors BOAC and the London *Daily Mirror*, they had kicking contests throughout the British Isles. The Patriots had gone along with the scheme, agreeing to guarantee a $25,000 contract for the eventual Superfoot. Hell, they could afford it the way they were selling tickets. Besides, our place kicking had been one of the more hopeless facets of our generally anemic offense.

Early that spring, Andelman, his cohorts, Billy Sullivan, and John Mazur embarked on their quest for the Holy Grail. After several weeks of scouring the British Isles they came up with three finalists, all of whom were signed to contracts and promised every opportunity to make the team in summer camp. While British commando sergeant Tug Wilson, Albie Booth, and the ultimate winner, bricklayer Mike Walker, did not stick with the team that year, a year later Walker would return for another shot in '72 and spend some time with the Patriots.

All was optimistic when we opened camp in Amherst. Upton Bell busied himself all summer wheeling and dealing bodies, energetically setting about repairing the tattered fragments of the previous year's disaster.

The regular season schedule facing us was imposing

enough. Besides two games each against the teams in our division (that's four games with Miami and Baltimore right there), we had to play Dallas, Cleveland, San Francisco, Detroit, Oakland, and Houston. With that undoubtedly in the back of his mind, Mazur, a former marine, instituted a boot camp atmosphere from the first day of camp.

We had to run an up-and-down-hill mile-and-a-half in an allotted time of twelve minutes. The nonqualifiers and dropouts had to run again until they made it.

In terms of personnel it was like a carousel. Players were grabbed off the waiver wire as soon as their names appeared. Five guys would get cut and three more would be brought to camp the same day. The press quickly dubbed it Bell's "revolving door policy," and the effect began to take its toll on the players as well. Nobody knew from one day to the next what the hell was going on. Not that Bell cared. He wanted to build the best team possible and reasoned that by looking over other teams' discards he had little to lose but the bus fare.

Players would sit around after the evening meetings and complain about Upton's Ferris wheel. Some guys never bothered to unpack their suitcases; they were staying prepared. The bus schedule to Hartford was posted in the lobby of our dormitory. Hartford offered the nearest jet service. Most people didn't need the bus, because they could usually catch a ride with one of the ball boys, who were constantly on the move to the Connecticut capital to pick up the latest gem plucked off the waiver wire.

The looniest times of all would come on days when there was a big roster cut scheduled. The scouts had been assigned the honor of informing the players whose services were no longer required. In the process they would also confiscate the hallowed playbook, although in our case, after a 2-12 season, God knows who could have wanted the thing.

Players would hide whenever a scout was spotted lurking suspiciously on a dorm floor. It was sort of a sadistic game of hide-and-seek. The scout would go looking for the guy, and when he flushed out the victim he was "it." And when you were "it" in this instance that usually meant it was all over, because when you'd been cut by the lowly Patriots you'd hit rock bottom.

When a man had been axed, tragically enough, he was usually completely shunned by the rest of his "former" teammates. Being cut makes you an instant leper.

One player who was virtually forgotten throughout training camp was Mike Taliaferro. He had been our starting quarterback until Kapp's arrival; in fact, at one time in his career he had played first string for the Jets. Joe Namath was his back-up. But now he was way in the background. The preseason prospectus issued by the team ran a picture of Kapp, Mazur, and Plunkett on the cover. Mike was being phased out, and he knew it. He was listed number three on the depth chart without having been given the slightest chance to win a job, while every publication in New England ran feature stories on our two heralded signal callers.

He was to get his revenge though. One day, unbeknownst to anyone, Joe Kapp vanished. The day before I'd given him a ride to the dorm in my car from practice. We'd talked of the arduous training camp, about winning and pride. A typical Kapp conversation. He appeared eager to atone for his rather mediocre showing in '70.

Now, suddenly, he was AWOL. The usual rumor mill started grinding them out at the rate of about five new ones an hour. Somebody said he'd been traded back to Minnesota. Another guy said he'd been traded even-up to the Jets for Joe Willie Namath. I heard another story that he'd been cut. One thing was certain though. Joe Kapp had moved out of his room and out of Amherst. Mike Taliaferro didn't say a word. He just smiled quietly.

A day later Mazur broke the news to the team. Kapp had left camp in a contractual dispute. Taliaferro's smile grew broader still. He still hadn't signed his '71 contract. Meanwhile, Kapp was advised by Pete Rozelle to stay away from Amherst until the matter was resolved. It never was, and he never came back. His career as a Patriot had lasted all of twelve games — one win and eleven losses.

*

Now the Patriot management was in real bind. Since Plunkett was still in camp with the College All-Stars, there were only three quarterbacks in camp, and two of them were rookies. Taliaferro was the only veteran in sight, and he wasted little time in calling renowned sports attorney Bob Wolfe in to begin negotiations on a new pact. After the abuse they'd heaped on him, Taliaferro was going to exact retribution at the bargaining table. And he did. They paid dearly, giving him a substantial raise.

There had never been any love lost between Kapp and Taliaferro, but if Mike ever ran across the guy after he signed that contract he'd have kissed him on the spot.

As two-a-days drudged on, players continued to roll in and out of Amherst with alacrity. "We will," said Bell, "do anything to improve our ball club. If it means bringing in two hundred guys, then that's what I'll do."

Slowly but surely the older players from 1970 began to disappear from view. Charlie Frazier, an eight-year veteran, went early. So did Jim "Earthquake" Hunt, who was forced to "retire." My old roommate Gary Bugenhagen also departed early, and before camp was over they would be joined by a whole host of returnees from the previous year.

*

On Saturday, July 31, we were hit with another bombshell. Our best player, all-purpose halfback Carl Garrett, had been traded along with a high draft choice to the Dallas Cowboys for controversial running back Duane Thomas, veteran guard Halvor Hagen, and rookie wide receiver Honor Jackson. The locker room was buzzing again.

Mazur was visibly upset by Bell's decision to trade Garrett, particularly for Thomas. Duane simply was not Mazur's type of player, and it brought about the first sign of open mistrust between the coach and the general manager. The rift would widen as the year progressed.

Reporters were swarming around the training camp like so many ants. The normally staid, conservative Patriot management responded by going instant Hollywood. Every day was a new adventure.

Thomas reported late and then displayed a disinclination for associating with the other players. The only one he talked to was Steve Kiner, a linebacker Bell had acquired a few weeks before from the Cowboys. Kiner had been Thomas' roommate in Dallas. But by this time, Thomas was already a celebrity. Every time he yawned it made the newspapers.

When he did show up for meetings, Duane was usually late. Mazur appeared to be trying his best to accept Thomas, but the vibrations were obvious. He was clearly losing his patience, and Thomas would respond by staring off into space during meetings, paying no attention to what was transpiring.

Thomas hadn't worked out with the Cowboys during his holdout there, so he wasn't suiting up for practices. He wore his sweats, jogged around the practice field, and occasionally stopped to gaze off into the Berkshires. After one evening practice Mazur kept Thomas to work on some basic techniques. When he instructed him to line up in a three-point stance, Thomas replied, "In Dallas we do it this way, so you can see the linebackers," and set himself in a two-point, hands-on-knees stance.

Mazur was incensed. "Here," he bellowed, "we do it *my* way. Get the hell off this field and pack up. You're finished!"

Duane Thomas' career as a Patriot had come to an abrupt end. He left that night. Now everyone was wondering what would happen next. Bell was furious with Mazur, who'd left him seemingly holding the bag, and he hastily tried to work out a strategy to salvage Garrett out of the deal. The Patriots had made the trade, after all, and now the coach had thrown Thomas out of camp.

Bell devised a plan whereby the Patriots charged that Thomas should have completed a psychological examination as part of his physical; if he was mentally unfit to play, the rationale went, then the trade could be medically invalidated. Of course, Thomas himself was nowhere to be found.

Bell found a sympathetic ear in Pete Rozelle. Possibly because he was still feeling guilt pangs after allowing former number one selection Phil Olsen to slip to the Rams (for compensation Rozelle had decreed he himself would determine later after evaluating Olsen's performance during the '71 season) because of a loophole in his contract, Rozelle interceded and ordered Cowboys president Tex Schramm to return Carl Garrett to New England. After an adjustment was made, the Patriots were allowed to keep Hagen and Jackson.

*

Hagen remained, but with mixed emotions. He'd naturally miss the virtually guaranteed play-off money he'd collected in Dallas, but he also looked forward to the opportunity to be a starter. He was, of course, confused by some of the methods the Patriots employed.

In addition to enjoying an ultramodern life-style, our trainer, Bill Bates, was infamous for his eleven-year practice of taping ankles stark naked except for a T-shirt. The first day Hagen practiced with the Patriots he sat on the table and nearly fell off when Bates seized his foot and thrust it squarely into his crotch. Then he started taping. Hagen was shocked. He didn't know whether to wiggle his toes or not. Bates, in turn, worried constantly about catching terminal athlete's foot on his organ.

*

Our opening exhibition against the Vikings had lost much of its luster with Kapp's departure, but it did mean a homecoming of sorts for our eleven-year veteran kicker Gino Cappelletti. The Duke hailed from Keewatin, Minnesota, and had attended the University of Minnesota. The game afforded his parents the opportunity to see him play for the first time in years. There was even an entire Cappelletti rooting section in the stands comprised of his friends and relatives.

Gino was humiliated to the utmost. He never played during the entire meaningless exhibition game! With all those people there to honor him, he wasn't even allowed to so much as kick off. With his pride, though, Cappy never said a word. I imagine he realized what he was going up against. The entire affair was handled in true Patriots' style.

*

Our opponents for the first game to be played in brand-new Schaefer Stadium were the New York Giants, our old friends. The stadium had been constructed in under a year's time and was heralded as "The Miracle at Foxboro."

When the Giants game rolled around, the stadium still wasn't quite completed, and it provided a memory no one who was there will ever forget. Little extras like toilets and running water, for instance, weren't ready, and by the third quarter if you had to use the bathroom — which many people did, since Schaefer Beer Company, which had cosponsored the stadium's construction to the tune of $1,000,000 in exchange for the use of its name, was pushing its product as hard as it could — you had to wade through half a foot of floating excrement. Workmen's tools, lumber, shavings, nails, tile, and wire were scattered throughout the premises.

In the locker room the urinals had been built so that they were five feet or so off the ground. You had to literally piss upward to hit the mark. They had to bring in portable steps for guys like Charlie Gogolak and Johnny Outlaw, who otherwise wouldn't have been able to reach them. The commodes were also elevated like thrones. It was like taking a crap on Mount Everest. Some of the guys even got airsick.

As I was dressing for the game I leafed through the inaugural program. It was filled with more of those flowery Billy Sullivan letters, including one thanking all the people connected with making Schaefer Stadium possible. The list included Dave McConnell and Bob Wetenhall, two of the stockholders who were deeply involved in a move to depose Sullivan as president. Reverse psychology, I suppose.

Before the game there was a tribute to Vince Lombardi, who had died of cancer. Sullivan had assembled about eight-dozen priests to take part. The field looked like it had suddenly been visited by a flock of penguins.

We managed to beat the Giants, thereby winning our first preseason game in two years. A wild locker room celebration followed, replete with postgame speeches, grab-ass, and war whoops. If that sounds like an excessive amount of jubilation over winning one lousy exhibition game, it probably was. But then, we hadn't had much to celebrate for a long time.

After taking a cold shower — hot water was among the items yet to be installed at the stadium — I headed for a party in downtown Boston. I never made it. There was a horrendous traffic jam outside the stadium. Thousands of cars were trapped inside the parking lot.

The Patriots had done it again. Despite all the careful planning that had gone into the construction of Schaefer Stadium, the necessity for access roads hadn't occurred to anyone. Only one trafficway, Route 1, passes by the Stadium, and cars were backed up for miles. Many motorists in despair simply left their cars where they were and took the train back to Boston. Many more cars overheated on the highway, and not a few ran out of gas. The New York Giants' bus was stuck in the parking lot.

The players were invited to a party hosted by the Patriot hierarchy in the clubhouse of the adjacent Bay State Raceway. After surveying the hopeless situation on the highway, I contemplated my consummate desire for a cold brew right then and decided to attend after all.

After three hours at the party I decided to call it a night and head back for my apartment. When I emerged from the racetrack what I encountered was stupefying. It was now two o'clock in the morning and the highway was *still* clogged up. The Giants were *still* in the parking lot. I stretched out and spent the night in my car.

*

The exhibition season crept on, and Schaefer Stadium presented new headaches each week. Prior to the Los Angeles game, the Foxboro Board of Health had threatened to shut the stadium down because of the chronically malfunctioning toilet system. The owners huddled and saved the day with a last-minute desperation effort. After hastily making the necessary repairs, the owners and employees assembled at the stadium and in an ingenious demonstration, simultaneously flushed every head in the joint. The board of health was satisfied and lifted the ban. The team's management breathed a sigh of relief. Not only would the game go on, but had their grand experiment failed, they could have suffered the same fate as the fans had at the New York game. Which is to say, they could have been bathed in excrement.

As the chinks in the armor continued to pop up, the psychological effect on the team was disastrous. After losing the Rams game, we were scheduled to play the Falcons next. Our locker room facilities were condemned by the board of health. There was so much alien dung floating around in the bathrooms that it was fit only for the thousands of flies who used it as a combination dining room and breeding ground.

We were dispatched to a local grade school to dress for the game, and the Patriots were naturally assigned the girls' locker room. Mike Taliaferro swished around on tiptoes, giving each player a new moniker. Bob Gladieux was now Roberta, Ed Philpott was Phyllis, and so on. The whole place had an atmosphere of, well, gaiety. Everyone was laughing and mincing around like a bunch of marshmallow faggots. Even the coaches thought it was funny. The Falcons didn't. They whipped us good.

Morale was already starting to ebb. The Atlanta loss was our third consecutive defeat and the seventeenth in our past twenty games. Things were hardly looking up.

Our final preseason game was against the Jets in Memphis. Two days before the game we'd picked up an old Bronco teammate of mine named Mike Haffner. In Denver he'd been known as "Scoop" because he always seemed to have the lowdown on everything. He was one of those guys who would never in a million years answer "I don't know" to a question.

Just before departure at Logan Airport, Haffner was shooting the shit with equipment manager George Luongo, and it came up in conversation that the Broncos had played an exhibition game against the Falcons in Memphis just a few weeks before. Luongo happened to ask Haffner what sort of turf the Memphis stadium had, and Scoop replied, "Astro-turf."

Luongo turned white as a ghost. He'd been informed by someone in Memphis that the field was grass, but obviously Haffner was in a position to know, having played there only three weeks before.

Ten minutes before takeoff, Luongo left and drove back to Foxboro to pick up our soccer shoes. All we had packed were cleats. He told us he'd catch the next plane.

When we arrived in Memphis we were taken directly to the field for a workout. The field was all natural grass. Scoop Haffner had come through again. I learned later that he hadn't even played in the Atlanta game and had forgotten what the turf was like. We were very nearly the first professional football team to have a murder on the field. The incident presaged the outcome of the game.

We stunk. The most exciting thing that happened in the game came when, midway through the second quarter, without calling a time out, Jimmy Cheyunski bolted off the field and ran at full speed for the locker room. It seems he was suffering from an acute attack of diarrhea and desperately needed to take a dump. The locker room door, naturally, was locked, and it was a race against time as George Luongo dashed from the bench with the keys to let him in.

Once again we got stomped, running our exhibition record to 1-5. I felt like joining Cheyunski in the head.

*

The coaches told us to forget the exhibition season and look ahead to the future. The games would count from now on. What else could they say? Meanwhile, training at Foxboro was unbearable. There was no running water, no shower facilities, no toilets, no drinking water. We dressed and showered at the Red Fox Motor Inn, down the road on Route 1. Some guys, shunning this, elected to drive home in full uniform and shower there.

Swarms of bees dive-bombed the field on a daily basis. There would be little or no water available in the ninety-degree heat, and since the turds were still floating around in the latrine there was no way for anyone to relieve himself. Finally they brought in a porta-john and installed it in front of the locker room entrance. Progress was being made, even if it meant relieving yourself in front of 60,000 gaping football fans.

The workmen slaved all week trying to get the stadium ready for the season opener against the Oakland Raiders. After all, the list of dignitaries scheduled to be present for the ballyhooed opening day festivities read like a *Who's Who of New England,* and if the toilets weren't working this time the Patriot management was going to come away with a lot of egg on its face.

The Raiders were favored to win the AFC title that year,

and in light of our spectacular record, we went off at anywhere from twenty- to thirty-five-point underdogs. Before the game our locker room was hushed and solemn. It was like being in a church; you could have easily gotten the impression that we were ready to play football. We were.

Players sat around reading the dedication day program. Dozens of letters graced the pages bidding Billy Sullivan and the Patriot family good luck. There were letters from President Nixon, the governors of the six New England states, various NFL owners, and Pete Rozelle. And naturally there was Sullivan's own flowery incantation, thanking everybody who had had anything to do with the construction of Schaefer Stadium as well as our masochistic season-ticket holders.

The sellout crowd of 61,000 was treated to a modern-day miracle. We beat the Raiders 20 to 6. It was hailed as the greatest day in the Patriots' history. Despite all the problems, miscalculations, malfunctions, and discomforts experienced by the players and coaches over the past weeks, we rose to the occasion and played a truly superb game. The locker room scene after the game was one of total frenzy.

Sullivan came around beaming with Senator Ed Brooke and greeted each player individually. Politicians and other influential people trooped in to offer their congratulations for the job we'd done against the Raiders. Fortunately, the plumbing had been repaired and the floor of the latrine mopped up.

❖

Over the course of that year the entire team did a remarkable job in overcoming the many obstacles and hindrances we faced. Besides the stadium crises, there was the continually growing strife between Bell and Mazur. After our miserable '70 season and our equally gloomy exhibition record, we should have been shoo-ins to repeat our finish in the NFL cellar; with the other pressures that beset us it should have been a certainty. But the players developed a solidarity among themselves and adjusted to the trying circumstances.

One of the more glaring problems involved a communications gap between defensive coordinator Dick Evans and the defensive players. Linebacker Fred Whittingham had nicknamed the coach "Big Bird," after the "Sesame Street" character, and it stuck throughout his stay in Foxboro.

After practice each day a dozen or so players would assemble at the nearby Red Snapper and discuss the day's proceedings. It eventually got so that most of the talk centered around Big Bird and his defense. Jim Cheyunski and Ricky Harris were two of Evans' most severe critics. It eventually got so that neither of them would even listen to him. They considered his coaching methods archaic, and with the passing of a few beers the stories got funnier and funnier.

One of the typical Big Bird incidents occurred during training camp. Evans, conducting a meeting, had rambled on for an hour or so, and some players were staring off into space, others nodding out in their chairs. At the end of the lengthy meeting he asked the players if they had any questions. A rookie defensive end named Hank Barton raised his hand. "What kind of sandwiches are going to be served at lunch?" Barton asked. The room roared hysterically.

Evans had a particularly tough time relating to Steve

Kiner, who was infamous for having a mind of his own and his own way of doing everything. He kept to himself most of the time and was quietly distant. During one meeting Kiner was staring at the ceiling, and Evans, conducting a blackboard session, repeatedly asked Kiner to look at him. Kiner wouldn't. He just kept staring at the ceiling as if he hadn't heard. Linebacker coach John Meyer almost threw Steve out of the room, and from then on Big Bird referred to Kiner only as "Stare Guy."

Evans also reinstituted the "Thursday Night Rule." The rule demands that a player abstain from sexual activity from Thursday night until after the game. Allegedly this would save all his strength for the game. I seriously doubt that anyone followed the rule. Trainer Bill Bates privately dismissed Evans' dictum as an "old wives'" tale and advised players to get all they could up until an hour before game time.

Evans had another rule: no saunas after Thursday. I never did figure out why, but we were barred from the sauna from Thursday on. Later in the season when the temperatures dropped, some players found it extremely difficult to maintain playing weights, yet Evans adamantly refused to let them shed a few pounds in the sauna room.

Emotionally our season ran in highs and lows. We'd knock off the teams who were supposed to beat us like Miami, Oakland, and Baltimore. Then we'd turn around and lose to supposedly inferior teams — Buffalo and the New York Jets.

Our erratic performance greatly displeased Upton Bell. If we could beat the Dolphins and the Raiders, he reasoned, why the hell couldn't we beat the Bills? Bell questioned Mazur's ability to motivate. The word was all over the locker room that Bell desperately wanted to bring in his own head coach; he clearly didn't want John Mazur running "his" ball club. It was no secret that he coveted Howard Schnellenberger, the top Dolphin assistant. He had done a remarkable job in the short time he'd been in New England, but he wanted to build the entire team his way, and Mazur and his staff were not included in his plans.

Mazur, for his part, resented Bell's arrogance and brash attitude, and as the year progressed several little incidents exacerbated the differences between the two.

During training camp Mazur had been vociferously critical of Bell's revolving door. He found it difficult to coach smoothly with new faces repeatedly turning up, and he considered Bell's constant influx of new material to be a hindrance to the team's progress. He and the other coaches also blamed Bell for the Phil Olsen episode, although Bell maintained that the loophole had stemmed from the malfeasance of a secretary — one who, incidentally, was no longer employed by the Patriots.

Then, before one game, Mazur made a tactical error when he revealed to the press that quarterback Dick Shiner's name was on the waiver list, thereby violating a league rule and causing Shiner to walk out of the New York Giants camp. Later in the year, after Bell had cleared a waiver deal with the Dallas Cowboys for wide receiver Reggie Rucker, the Giants retaliated by grabbing Rucker before he could get through to the Patriots. Out of spite, they held him for several weeks before releasing him to the Patriots. Bell was incensed by the entire episode and criticized Mazur for "a lack of professionalism." Lack of professionalism or not, it cost the coach a stiff fine from the league office.

During the season Bell would occasionally stroll out onto the practice field to watch us in workouts. Some assistant coaches would sneer to one another, "Here comes Napoleon" and "I wonder where his white horse is today? Maybe he left it on Broadway." There was clearly no love lost between Bell and any of the coaching staff. It was a case of mutual disrespect.

Conditions at the stadium were gradually rectified as the season progressed. The plumbers came in and ripped out the urinals and commodes and lowered them to a more reasonably attainable height. They did miscalculate slightly, so the latrine now resembled a bathroom for midgets, but at least you didn't have to hook yourself up to a garden hose to take a leak.

Meetings would be continually interrupted by workmen pounding hammers, sawing boards, or walking in and out carrying building materials. Meetings were also occasionally interrupted by Harpo Gladieux's rather pungent crepitations. More than once he cleared out an entire section of the meeting room with a single fart. Then he'd sit back and bask in his glory while everyone else flayed him with every name in the book.

But Gladieux wasn't the only player suffering from gastrohypertension. The problem was eventually traced to the lady who operated a lunch wagon in Foxboro. Every day she'd pull up in front of the stadium gate, and players would flock to her truck to buy lunch. About two hours later the ill effects would begin to take effect, and it got so that the offensive huddle smelled like a plugged-up sewer. On a hot, humid day, it was all but unbearable.

Ptomaine Mary, as the players affectionately called the lady, only lasted a few months. She pushed her luck too far and took to parking her lunch wagon in the stadium parking lot before Sunday games to peddle her greaseburgers. The people who ran the stadium concession didn't appreciate the competition. They ran her out of Schaefer faster than you could say food poisoning. After Ptomaine Mary's banishment the guys started brown-bagging it again and the air around the stadium was purified once more.

✳

One advantage to playing for a team no one expects to go anywhere is that the atmosphere is always loose. Our locker room in '71 was very loose. Sure, the coaches were on Bell's chopping block and they knew it, but the team in general was enjoying the unaccustomed luxury of winning a few games. Winning with the Patriots at all was an almost unheard-of phenomenon.

Our squad had a little bit of everything. We had instant superstars like Jim Plunkett, who was voted the AFC's rookie of the year, and Julius Adams, who also made the All-Rookie team, and Damon Runyon types like minuscule Randy Vataha (Plunkett's teammate from Stanford, whom we'd picked up after he'd been cut by the Rams; he was tiny enough to have worked one summer at Disneyland, playing one of the seven dwarfs), and "Superfly," Hubie Bryant, whose dress was strictly out of the pages of *Clockwork Orange.* We even won two games in a row at one point, and then three out of five. For the first time the local papers were predicting great things in the future for the Patriots.

The problem with instant success, in our case, was that some players were ill equipped to handle it. They were so used to being the dogs of the NFL that after a win they would celebrate for days. Not a few players lived out of cars, spending their time in local bars and returning home only occasionally to change their underwear.

Every day the sauna would be filled with players who'd come to sweat off the previous night's booze, and the conversations invariably turned to who had slept with whom, where, and how many times. It was like a gigolos' convention every afternoon. If you believed them, Don Juan and Casanova had nothing compared to the New England Patriots.

Each win would leave us in a poor frame of mind for the upcoming games, a malady that beset us throughout the year. One week we'd be fantastic, clobbering a tough opponent like the Dolphins, and a week later we'd stink up the field. It was simply a question of mental preparation, but we'd be so engrossed in savoring a win that practice would be lackadaisical and distracted.

The offensive linemen had a year-long contest to see who would jump offside the most times during the course of the season. Halvor Hagen and Bill Lenkaitis were the scorekeepers. On one occasion during practice the offense broke the huddle and ran to the line of scrimmage. Hagen suddenly forgot the count and whispered to Lenkaitis, who was playing center on the series of downs, "What's the count?"

"On one, one," replied Lenk.

As Plunkett barked out the signals Hagen exploded into

the defensive line at the count of one. The count, of course, had been two. Devious methods. But Lenkaitis was laughing so hard he couldn't snap the ball, and the rest of the linemen were laughing nearly as hard too. Mazur, irate, called us a bunch of donkeys and made us run the play over.

As the offside contest neared the final few weeks it began to get totally ridiculous. Hagen, Lenkaitis, and I would line up and give fake snap counts. I would say it was on three, Hagen on one, and Lenkaitis on four. Invariably we'd induce some poor rookie to jump offside in the confusion. Plunkett even dropped back on the wrong count once. Hagen eventually won the contest with a dozen or so offsides; he pulled a George C. Scott and refused to accept his award.

Another contest, the Annual New England Berry Festival, was held in the locker room. Players were judged by the number of pimples on their asses. There were three categories, Most Berries, Largest Berries, and Most Improved Berries. Between heavy sweating, abrasions caused by rough football pants, and the humid weather, pimples on your derrière spread like wildfire. A guy could have a baby-smooth bum one day and the next day look like he'd been hit with birdshot at point-blank range. The race stayed close all year between Gladieux, St. Jean, and Rick Cash, although occasionally Lenkaitis would have a tough day and make a strong bid.

At the end of the season the finalists were posted on the bulletin board and the entire squad voted for the Berry King. In a close race, Bob Gladieux narrowly won the coveted Strawberry Fields Award.

*

Some of the more intellectual players, though, looked upon the Berry Contest with disdain, if not contempt. They preferred to pass their time in the locker room with more socially relevant pursuits. One time, for instance, Mike Taliaferro and Bill Bates ruffled through some of the many letters Billy Sullivan had written for various programs to see who could come up with the letter with the most first person singular pronouns. At the end of the year Bates's winning letter was posted on the bulletin board. It contained a total of thirty-eight "I's" and "Me's."

The future of the coaching staff was still in doubt going into the final game. Everyone in New England was aware that Upton Bell desperately wanted to rid himself of Mazur and his staff, but our record was 5-8, decidedly mediocre, but such a vast improvement over the previous campaign that people were seriously talking about Mazur as a candidate for Coach of the Year.

In our last game in Baltimore, we knocked off the play-off–bound Colts, 21-17, and the coaches breathed a sigh of relief. The saviors were, in this instance, Jim Plunkett and the 5'9" dwarf, Randy Vataha, who caught an eighty-eight-yard bomb late in the fourth quarter on a play improvised in the huddle.

In the midst of the insanity on the flight back to Boston I couldn't help but wonder about the fate of Mike Taliaferro. He hadn't played a single down on offense all year. Plunkett had been the signal caller for every single offensive play, an unprecedented feat in the history of the NFL. Mike had been used only as a holder for place kicks.

The champagne flowed freely all the way back. We'd had a lot of fun during the season, and you'd have to have been

around in the midst of despair the year before to know just
how good we felt after a 6-8 season. It was the best record
of any team I'd ever played for.

I was already looking ahead to '72. After five years of losing, I was confident that we had finally turned the corner,
that this was indeed a team of the future. Plunkett, I was
sure, would be even better with a year's experience under
his belt, and I was already thinking of play-offs and Super
Bowl checks to come. Christmas, I thought, had come early.
Just thinking about next year with Plunkett, Vataha, Kiner,
and Adams would keep me warm all winter long.

9

Banned in Boston

WHATEVER ELSE might have been said about the Patriots, there could be no denying that we stuck together. We won a few together, lost a lot together, and, off the field, drank — drank one hell of a lot, in fact — together. The rapport and camaraderie professional athletes maintain with one another is an iron bond, a mutual respect for ability and sheer survival in the NFL. If there were personal rivalries and jealousies, which are inevitable, they were left on the practice field. If there was dissension on the Patriots, it certainly didn't extend to the forty-man playing roster.

Just before the last preseason game in early September 1970 Houston Antwine, our player rep, requested that we assemble and drive, caravan-style, to a recording studio in South Boston. Some genius had cooked up a project wherein each NFL team would record an album of Christmas songs to be sold in its respective area, with the NFL's cut of the residuals to go directly to the Players' Association. The "Holiday Halftime" albums would be sold at some point, presumably before the Yuletide season.

Some of the guys demurred, on the very logical grounds that after a hard day's practice they would be very much in need of food and liquid sustenance and hardly in a mood for Christmas caroling on a hot Indian summer evening. "Twine" assured us that there would be an ample supply of beer and sandwiches provided by the studio. If that didn't exactly placate everyone, it did, at least, more or less squelch all possible lines of refusal, and we assembled at the studio for our musical debut.

The food and beer were set out to greet us on our arrival. Lots of food and beer. The guys were devouring the stuff, cramming sandwiches in their mouths and sloshing it down with beer while the album's associate producer, Jack French, briefed us on the recording procedure. French had been Liza Minnelli's personal conductor, which impressed me, but most of the players were too busy with the refreshments to care much.

He explained that the album idea had been conceived by Mike Tatick and Jacques Urbont. Urbont, better known as the composer for the scores to TV greats like "Mission Impossible" and "Mannix," no doubt cringes today at the very mention of "Holiday Halftime" in conjunction with his own name. At the very best, it was horrendous. It should have been left in the can and used as the soundtrack for *The Exorcist* several years later.

We were supposed to record nine songs over the course of six hours. First, French and an accompanist on piano quickly ran through the arrangement, and then we tried. We were awful. You could hear resounding throughout the room a chorus of flat notes, loud beer farts, and off-key belches. It took us fully two hours to croon our way through "Winter Wonderland" and "Frosty the Snowman." French kept trying to encourage us by telling us we sang a lot better than the Vikings or the Redskins. By then it was getting dark and several of the players were developing itchy feet in anticipation of hitting the streets, and finally a dual case of attrition set in, with some players sneaking out the door while others, still in the studio, began to succumb to the beer. Bull Bramlett, who had the best voice among the white players, volunteered for a solo on "All I Want for Christmas Is My Two Front Teeth," and while his singing wasn't bad, the background consisted mostly of laughter, slurred words, chug-a-lugging, and general chaos. We'd have gotten thrown out of Morey's in New Haven on that night.

Eventually we were down to about sixteen voices. One of the guys had puked in the back of the studio and quietly returned to his seat in the chorus, with everyone save the fellow sitting next to him oblivious to this act of degradation. Another fell asleep in the corner. Johnny Outlaw, Daryl Johnson, and Clarence Scott were by then the only players in the joint who could utter a sober note, and they were determined to sing soul renditions of the Yuletide standards. Poor Jack French was going nuts. When we finally wrapped up the session at 11:00 P.M., the players who could still walk carried out the players who couldn't. French undoubtedly ran to the nearest bar for a double.

A couple of months later we were each presented with a copy of "The Patriots Sing: Holiday Halftime." I was apprehensive, with good reason, when I opened the LP and put it on the turntable. It was awful. The only cuts that wouldn't make a dog howl in pain were the ones on which they'd added studio voices. In most cases not even *that* helped. The album sold perhaps a half-dozen copies.

*

A month or so later that year, in order to promote that nebulous concept known as "team unity," a few of the veteran players came up with the idea of a get-together after Tuesday practice. Everyone was asked to chip in five bucks to cover the cost of beer and food at a place in the suburbs run by a friend of Bramlett's and Ed Philpott's.

We had a 100 percent turnout, and the owner was immensely hospitable, ushering us through the lounge and downstairs to the party room, where there was a keg of beer and a buffet of cold cuts, cheese, bread, and the customary garnishes. It was convivial enough at first, but scarcely an hour had passed before some of the guys were filtering out, in some cases to go home but more often than not to find some spot offering female companionship, distinctly absent at the party.

Fifteen or so of us hung around shooting the bull, with Joe Kapp more or less chairing the gathering, regaling us with tall tales of romanticism and chivalry. By then the food had long since run out and the beer tap was spewing foam; all that remained was a giant chunk of Swiss cheese. We requested more beer. The owner returned with a case of Budweiser and proceeded to ask us to pay for it. He should have known better.

By then the only people in attendance were the more serious drinkers, and while we were stunned and perhaps hurt, we were generally pissed off after laying out $200 for a keg of beer and a bunch of cold cuts. Len St. Jean put the beer in the ice that the keg had sat in, and we sat around sulking and grumbling. Someone suggested a poker game, which seemed as good a thing as any under the circumstances. We were given a deck of cards, but when we were asked for seventy-five cents to pay for them, the atmosphere became ominous.

Ron Berger, at 6'8" and 280 pounds one of the biggest men in pro football, angrily snatched a beer out of the tub and flopped back into his folding chair. It collapsed into pieces under him. We burst out laughing, but it wasn't really laughter. It was a sort of maniacal cackle from the depths of the demented. Emulating Berger, I rose up and jumped back into my chair, which also shattered, and the siege was on. Within seconds the place was in utter chaos. Somebody grabbed the cheese and started a game of hot potato, which soon evolved into a punting contest. Most of the cheese wound up sticking to the ceiling.

The room was demolished with a vengeance. With the stragglers in the poker game seemingly oblivious, foreign objects flew about. Glasses, ashtrays, and cheese crashed off the walls. Bill Rademacher, a former member of the Jets, took off his Super Bowl ring under the pressure of some strong needling from Kapp and tossed it into the mayonnaise bowl. Len St. Jean lifted up the tub of ice water and dumped it over Philpott's head. By then the piano was in dire jeopardy, with guys hurling it against the wall, eliciting all manner of eerie chords, while there were a couple of inches of water and beer covering the floor, on which floated playing cards and bits of cheese. The chef had joined the merriment, and when the outraged owner, summoned by the noise, came downstairs and began to bellow, the chef promptly threw him out of the room. Discretion being the better part of valor, we decided to split. Hell, if we'd done to other NFL teams what we did that night we'd have gone undefeated that year.

The next day the papers were filled with accounts of the havoc. "Patriots Finally Become Aggressive," read one headline. "Pats Make Contact," said another. Before practice Bramlett received a phone call in the locker room. It was his friend, and all I could hear on his end of the conversation was a steady stream of "Yes sir, no sir, yes sir," not normally consistent with Bramlett's vocabulary. The restaurant owner apparently was threatening everything from lawsuits to capital punishment unless we made restitution for what he claimed to be $400 in damages. We were taking so much abuse from the fans and the press as it was that it seemed propitious to comply. The chief culprits came up with $20 each, and a few other participants chipped in $10, adding up to about $200. Kapp contributed the rest. He'd enjoyed himself so much he was actually happy to part with the $200. The evening was unquestionably the highlight of the season.

*

By the next year our team parties had become more or less a weekly ritual, as many of the players celebrated for days, if not a full week at a time, and Daisy Buchanan's, a Back

Bay bar partly owned by hockey player Derek Sanderson, became our usual Tuesday haunt. Our new progressive general manager Upton Bell even encouraged the team parties,
giving team captain Jon Morris a weekly check to cover the
cost. Bell also subscribed to the theory that players who
practice together, play together, and drink together will
weld a bond of solidarity that will eventually lead to winning together. Unfortunately some of the wives didn't see it
that way, and when they heard of some of the escapades at
"that den of iniquity" they threatened their husbands with a
permanent Thursday night rule à la Dick Evans if they attended, with the result that there was a standard absentee
rate of about 25 percent — almost all of it among the mar-
ried players. For the single players who lived near the stadium in Foxboro, on the other hand, the weekly foray to
Daisy's was akin to being turned loose in a Nevada brothel,
and since a man can grow some long, fuzzy horns living
down in no man's land, the occasional secretaries and
stewardesses who wandered into Daisy's by mistake on a
Tuesday night often needed track shoes and a can of Mace
to get out.

One evening Jack Maitland, one of our running backs, was
on the loose. Jack is your classic swinging single pro athlete:
intelligent, good-looking, a Williams graduate who drives a
Porsche. Tuesday nights he was invariably on the prowl
from the minute he walked in the door. On this particular
evening he got hammered very early and spent most of it
unsuccessfully scouring the place for a roommate. As the
wee hours approached, the place had pretty much thinned
out, most of the chicks having departed. The hangers-on

looked like Secretariat. At long last, the bleary-eyed
Maitland spotted one in the corner. She was a real trophy,
who had an obsession about hockey players, but in a pinch a
football player would do.

She showed up at Daisy's week in and week out wearing
the same clothes. I seriously doubt that she ever washed
them, much less herself, but in his condition Maitland found
her quite attractive. I saw him walk out the door with her,
but I didn't say anything.

The next day he showed up at practice with a very embarrassed and contrite expression on his face. I asked him how
it had gone.

"Driving home," he said, shaking his head, "I started to
notice this peculiar odor. I thought I was downwind from
the ocean at low tide, sort of a putrid aroma. I looked next
to me and suddenly sobered up. I couldn't believe I'd
grabbed this one. I opened my window and the cold air
really straightened me out. I panicked." I was cracking up
while Maitland recounted the details of how he'd abruptly
informed his "date" that his bad knee was suddenly acting
up and that he'd better drop her off and immediately go see
the team doctor. At one in the morning yet. Jack said he
had to fumigate his car after she got out. I told him he'd
learned a lesson: never mess around with hockey players'
women.

❋

Later on that season at another Tuesday night bash Lenny
St. Jean and Bill Lenkaitis decided to kill a bottle of tequila
with beer chasers. I watched them sit and talk, laughing
about practice and the coaches and generally have a good

time. Then they were suddenly sitting frozen on their stools like a pair of statues. I ordered a drink, turned around, and they'd both vanished. I searched the room for them and eventually found Lenk sitting nonchalantly on the floor, head bowed, staring into an enormous pool of puke. He had a silly little grin on his face and when I asked him if he was O.K. he giggled, tried to speak, and threw up all over himself again. He finally recovered enough to leave.

I finally found Lenny. He was sitting on the toilet in the men's room, fully clothed and soaking wet from sweating. I led him out of the john and decided he'd better sleep it off at my apartment a block away. I pushed him into my bed and returned to Daisy's. I got back home about two and crashed on my couch. When I woke up around eight in the morning I was overwhelmed with a very unfriendly, pungent sort of stench. With severe trepidation I opened my eyes and discovered that poor Lenny, waking up in the middle of the night, had tried to make it to the bathroom to blow lunch. Unfortunately it had been too dark to find his way, with the result that the carpet, walls, woodwork, and furniture were all decorated with the previous night's menu. That marked the last time I benevolently lent my bed to a fallen comrade.

❋

By the next season Upton Bell had cut off the party funds, and things on the Tuesday night circuit generally went downhill, just as the team's fortunes did. Upton claimed that the collective bargaining agreement between the owners and the Players' Association forced the elimination of such practices. We had a few soirees provided gratis by the people at Daisy's, and were honored as well by a sister club,

Zelda's, which opened that year. Zelda's was a real trip. Most of the clientele were generally spaced-out girls who wouldn't have cared much about football players if they knew what one was, preferring instead to make it with some greasy five-foot midget in eight-inch platform shoes. Not, for the most part, our type of groupie. Prospects in the place were so grim, in fact, that at one team party that happened to coincide with Jim Plunkett's birthday someone had to bribe a girl to be Jim's birthday present. He'd slipped a chick a few bucks to make sure she'd show Jim a good time. Plunkett, while not exactly a prude, is basically a pretty shy guy, though, and this was exacerbated by the fact that in attendance at the party that night was Larry Fox of the New York *Daily News,* who was doing a book on Jim. Plunkett spent more time that night running from her than he did scrambling away from a pass rush on any given Sunday. The poor girl finally gave up in frustration. "I can't help it," she said with tears in her eyes. "I can't corner him."

On another night at Zelda's one of our players drew the attention of a seedy-looking blonde. He talked with her for a while at the bar, bought her a drink, and the next thing I knew they were on the dance floor. One of the regulars I knew quietly approached me and whispered, "See that blonde dancing out there?" I nodded. "Well, she's a he." I almost died. I quickly apprised my teammate of the information. He vanished into the night.

❋

In the midst of the turmoil in '72 our morale was at rock bottom. A friend of mine named Dick "Moose" Moskoff de-

cided to toss a party for the team at his downtown Boston
club, Chez Moose. He had flyers printed up proclaiming,
"Let's bring back the Pats with a pat on the back." (At that
point we were the laughingstock of both the football world
and all of New England.) Moskoff scheduled the bash during the same week Phil Bengtson took over as interim coach,
and he'd asked me to distribute the flyers to the players at
practice — a little something to show the guys that in spite
of a rotten year a lot of people still cared.

Bengtson happened to chance on one of the flyers in the
locker room and immediately ordered the players not to attend. "You guys have to start thinking about the game on
Friday, not Sunday, but Friday. A function like this is going
to be detrimental to your performance on Sunday. Stay
home and get some rest." Fat chance. That night about
half the team showed up and had a great time. A commer-
cial artist had heard about Bengtson's edict and drawn up a
huge poster, a caricature of Bengtson using his head on a
small body carrying a water bucket. The caption was
saying, "52-0!! Vince Lombardi would puke!!" (That happened to be the score of our loss the preceding weekend.)
In bold letters above the headshot of Bengtson was the
phrase, "If this man shows up, blow the whistle. He is not
invited!" Around the neck hung a genuine ocarina, waiting
to be tooted. The poster cracked up everyone, including
the twenty-odd players attending, who by then sure needed
some kind of lift. I realized that it was the first time I'd
heard them laugh in days.

10

Join the Patriots' Revolution

I'D NEVER EXPERIENCED an off season like the one that followed. Endorsements, speaking engagements, and all manner of optimistic prognoses by the media followed our "successful" '71 campaign. Speaking engagements rolled in at the rate of two a week, and I was awarded the "Unsung Hero Award" by the 1776 boosters club. It had certainly been *my* most satisfying season in five years.

In a move that smacked of compromise, John Mazur was rehired, but only for one year. He'd received some votes for AFC coach of the year, and I thought he deserved them. Other teams were interested in him, reportedly Denver and Buffalo, and the word was that Mazur would have rejected the insulting one-year, no-confidence offer had he not been concerned over the fate of his assistants. To reject the job would have put them all out of work.

*

With all sorts of speculation going on about who the Patriots would select in the draft, they surprised everyone at the last minute by trading the number one pick to the

Giants for defensive end Fred Dryer. Upton Bell explained that Dryer was a better football player than anyone who would have been available at that point in the draft. Unfortunately, what he didn't explain was that no one had consulted Dryer about the deal, and Fred (who almost immediately had "free spirit" welded onto his name in its every appearance in print) happened to have played out his option in New York.

The upshot of all this was that if Bell couldn't sign Dryer by May he would be a free agent, on his own to make a deal for himself — which is exactly what happened. Fred went to the Rams, and the Patriots received — under the "Rozelle Rule" — compensation from Los Angeles in return. Not that it seemed particularly earthshaking at the time, but needless to say the board of directors did not paste any little gold stars next to Upton's name over *that* episode.

*

Then in May the coaches brought us all in for evaluation, primarily to check on what sort of shape we were in. (By now it was becoming fashionable for NFL teams to do this with veterans each spring.) Players who hadn't seen each other all winter were brought in from all over the country and assembled in Foxboro on a Saturday afternoon. After Mazur welcomed us we went through perfunctory physicals that lasted about thirty seconds each, took IQ tests (I guess they wanted to know if we'd gotten any dumber during the off season), and then had the rest of the night off. The guys were primed for hell-raising, and Boston swung till 5:00 A.M. Sunday.

When we reported to the stadium the next day there were

5000 fans on hand just to watch forty glassy-eyed veterans do chin-ups, dips, forty-yard dashes, and run a twelve-minute race! God, were we up. We were almost looking forward to training camp!

*

When we reported to Amherst that summer there were several trade rumors, some that truthfully couldn't even be described as rumors. Some veterans, including Jim Nance and Mike Taliaferro, were instructed not to even bother to show up. Steve Kiner was having all sorts of problems. He claimed he was hurt and couldn't scrimmage; he'd jog around the practice field in shorts and sweats while everyone else worked out. Mazur, who'd never had any great love for Steve in the first place, began to openly question the seriousness of Kiner's groin pull, and to make matters worse Steve was involved in a contract dispute with Bell and hadn't signed yet. Mazur finally got fed up and traded — or, more accurately, *gave* — the free spirit who'd been an AFC Defensive Player of the Week the year before to Miami for some guy named Bill Griffin. Griffin lasted a week.

Ron Sellers also departed. The coaching staff found Sellers, a one-time number one pick, a severe disappointment. There was no question about his talent, but he had acquired a rap in some quarters as being somewhat deficient in the guts department. He seemed to have more-than-usual difficulties when it came to catching balls in traffic or hanging onto them when he was tackled. He had also developed an incredible proclivity for getting hurt and was injured so frequently that even his teammates began to wonder. After one injury some of the guys on the team chipped in and sent him a dozen red roses and a get-well card. Sellers wasn't amused. He was traded to Dallas.

Our exhibition season was, to say the least, weird. We won two and lost four. When we lost we were rotten; when we won we looked like supermen. Bell's revolving door policy was still very much in evidence, and Mazur wasn't exactly pleased. The coach would have preferred to cut the squad down to a workable size and stress timing and fundamentals. Instead, new bodies would appear and disappear on a daily basis. As usual the Patriots were a windfall for the Peter Pan Bus Company in Amherst.

*

Much of the diversion at the '72 camp was provided by the rookie crop. Most of them couldn't play much football, but they were extremely gifted in other areas. Tight end John Nelson was an accomplished magician; safety Jeff Kolberg ate glass à la Tim Rossovich, and three other first-year men excelled in "free fall" jumping.

Each evening after supper Nelson would perform card tricks, handkerchief sleight-of-hand numbers, rope gimmicks — he had a repertoire of over a hundred magic tricks in his act. Unfortunately he hadn't yet devised a number that would keep him off the waiver list, and one night he was nowhere to be found after the evening meal. The veteran players expressed their displeasure over the magician's departure. "They should have kept him around and made him a ball boy or something," someone said.

Kolberg, a free agent from Oregon State, delighted the

crowds at local watering holes. More than once he shocked a waitress right out of her miniskirt when he ordered a glass, period, and then devoured it on the spot. He, too, took a hike midway through the preseason.

Two more rookies earned their traveling papers when they tried to sneak out of the dorm one night for a late date via the drainpipe. They tore it right off the wall and fell two stories to the rocky ground below. They were in no shape to even make the dates.

*

The evolution of male-female relationships at training camp never ceases to amaze me. The reason teams are sequestered so far in the middle of nowhere is nominally to discourage these diversions, a purpose that is, of course, unrealistic. But local girls of all shapes, sizes, and weights develop into beauty queens after four or five weeks. After two or three beers they look great. Unfortunately, even the porcine types were smart enough to know that they were the only females around, and they'd play hard to get. It was amazing listening to some of the bullshit lines guys would lay on these beasts. What a man won't do when he's desperate.

There was one girl who was a real trip. She would hang around the players night after night, but when it came down to the question of putting out it was invariably shutout time. What was amazing about her was that she was a walking storehouse of information about the players and the team, the internal workings of the club. No one could figure out how this local yokel, who didn't know beans about anything else, had acquired her expertise. It was finally discovered that she was "dating" a high-echelon individual in the organization. She wasn't as dumb as I'd supposed. A football player might be more glamorous, but there's a lot more security in the front office.

*

Our prospects for a winning season appeared excellent. A local sports publication called *Sports Record Weekly* had picked us to finish second in the division — ahead of Miami. The Boston *Herald-American* ran a full-page feature containing Upton Bell's "unbiased" explanation of how and why the Patriots would win. According to Upton the issue was remarkably uncomplicated: We were going to kick some ass for a change.

Plunkett, he said, was due for an even better season than his rookie year. Our receivers and running backs were vastly improved. The pieces were falling into place. Bell even flatly said we'd be anywhere from 7-7 to 9-5. The implication was clear: the play-offs were within reach. Bell, at least, was ready. It was up to the coaches to produce.

*

Rumblings of trouble between Bell and Mazur became louder and louder. The friction was apparent at training camp, where the two appeared to loathe the sight of one another. They rarely sat at the same table at meals and would each leak thinly veiled "off-the-record" information uncomplimentary to the other to the media. The whole situation was obviously unhealthy for the team. It appeared that the younger players preferred Bell's act, while, for the most part, the veterans tended to stick behind Mazur, the old pro.

There were guys coming and going all summer right up until the end. Going into the final week of the exhibition season there were over sixty players still in camp, over a dozen above the limit. The time for the final cut made for a rather spectacular scene. Coaches were frenetically running around all over the place, weeding out players as fast as they could. Some of them stationed themselves at the entrance of the locker room and lay in wait for their quarry.

One guy who was caught completely off guard was linebacker Billy Hobbs. Obtained from the Eagles in an off-season trade, Hobbs had moved into Kiner's vacated weak-side spot and stayed there throughout the exhibition season. He'd confidently had his bride of four months and his dog fly to Boston and had rented a house near Plymouth. Linebacker coach John Meyer was waiting for him. Hobbs was stunned.

You accept the fate of getting the ax when you're a benchwarmer, but when you're a *starter?* No one could understand it. Jim Cheyunski was in a rage. "Those idiots are completely out of their fuckin' *minds,"* he seethed, pointing toward the coaches' room. "I can't believe it. He was playing as well as anybody else." Hobbs, hurt and embarrassed, quietly slipped out of town.

Another player who went that day was Charlie Gogolak. Charlie had been running neck and neck all summer in a battle for the place-kicking job with Englishman Mike "Superfoot" Walker, and the contest, according to most observers, was a stalemate. Perhaps the Patriots wanted to get some mileage out of the publicity from the competition, but many of us couldn't help but feel that the fact that Gogolak's salary was considerably larger than Superfoot's was a major factor in the decision.

Charlie made the rounds in the locker room, shaking hands and saying goodbyes. He seemed oddly unconcerned about going on the waiver list, almost relieved. He was one of the first to grasp reality and perceive that everything portended something ominously rotten in Foxboro.

*

To the rest of us, the upcoming season still looked like the fulfillment of our dreams, and we were keyed up for the opener at home against the Bengals. Unlike '71, Schaefer Stadium was operating properly; we weren't, for once, coming off a disastrous season; and our schedule, while not exactly a "piece of pie" was nowhere near as brutal as the one we'd gone 6 and 8 with a year earlier.

Paul Brown did it to us again. The twenty-five-mph crosswind was ferocious, which always does wonders for a pass-minded offense; Plunkett's game was thrown off completely. Brown, on the other hand, elected to keep the ball on the ground, and Essex Johnson, Fred Willis, and Doug Dressler destroyed our defensive line as they methodically ran straight at — and through — it. We were hopelessly beaten and once again, said some, hopelessly outcoached. As we pointed for the Atlanta game a week hence the rumors abounded: If Mazur lost to the Falcons as he had to the Bengals he was gone. With a shot at a winning season, Upton wasn't about to let it slip away.

Perhaps Rockne was up there interceding with the angels

on behalf of old Notre Dame, but Mazur was spared again. For absolutely no explicable reason, Atlanta kicker Bill Bell lined up for a straight-ahead, ten-yard field goal with only ten seconds on the clock and the Falcons down by two. It was, very simply, nothing more than an extra point. He missed it. It wasn't blocked, he just shanked the ball off to the side. Choke. The place went bughouse, and the reprieved Mazur was beside himself with joy. Or relief.

The players were filing into the locker room in jubilant celebration past the writers, who'd already assembled outside. Len Frisoli, the head of security at Schaefer Stadium, holds the same post at a notorious East Boston racetrack, Suffolk Downs. As Len approached the locker room door one cynical reporter cracked, "Frisoli, if this had happened at Suffolk Downs, you'd have a team of agents investigating it already!"

*

But if the conclusion of the Atlanta game was freaky, it was only a tune-up for one of the more bizarre finishes in football history the next week. Playing the Washington Redskins, who went on to the Super Bowl that year, in Foxboro, we led 24-21 with only a couple of minutes left, and on fourth down Curt Knight tied the game up for the Skins with a field goal from inside the thirty. We were called for roughing the holder, Sonny Jurgensen, on the play, and rather than take the points, cantankerous George Allen elected to take the penalty, move the ball closer, and try for the win — with the tie to fall back on.

Our defense held, and on fourth down — again — Knight

set up for the field goal, this time from closer range. He missed it. We took over on our twenty, and this time Washington held. We had to punt with less than a minute left, and lo and behold, Pat Studstill's kick was blocked. The Redskins' Bill Malinchak fell on the ball in the end zone, then slid out of the end zone for what was either a Washington touchdown or a safety against us. After a lengthy conference and much protestation, the officials ruled that Malinchak hadn't had *possession* of the ball while still in the confines of the end zone and that it was therefore a safety.

With the score now 24-23 we had to kick to Washington, and the Redskins maneuvered themselves into position for Knight to try one more field goal with a couple of seconds left. He missed that one too. It was incredible. Within the last two minutes of the game, we had the potential to — subject only to the accuracy of their place kicker, the decision of their coach, and the whim of the officials — win, tie, lose, tie, win, lose, win, lose, and finally, win. Ironically, the margin of victory was provided by a Charlie Gogolak field goal. Superfoot had torn a thigh muscle the week before, and Gogo had been reactivated.

Once again Mazur's tenure for the balance of the season, at least, appeared secure. While in truth we'd done less to win the two games than the opposition had to lose them, we were on cloud nine again. Reporters were once again conceding the possibility of a winner in Foxboro, and some of the guys were already dividing up their play-off loot. Billy Sullivan wore a perpetual smile. Upton Bell, his prediction of a winning season seemingly vindicated, was higher than a kite. The Washington game was even featured on the CBS "Game of the Week."

For once we were indeed kicking somebody else's butt instead of playing doormat. Practices were loose, and there was lots of merriment and clowning around. One afternoon flanker Hubie Bryant showed up for practice wearing calf-high red sneakers. Even the coaches laughed. We had reason to be hanging loose; after posting a winning record against two tough teams, we faced a breather the next week in the struggling Buffalo Bills.

✱

For the first time in six years I actually saw the sun in Buffalo. I could hardly believe it. As we jogged through our pregame warm-ups, players were joking about that big foreign object in the sky. Was it a UFO? In Buffalo you normally get rain, snow, sleet, or hail, or any combination of the above, but *never* the sun. I felt rather uneasy. I wasn't even sure how you're *supposed* to play in the sun in Buffalo. The equipment man even leaves the eye shadow home.

Former trainer Bill Bates once asked one of the Bills how much he hated the city of Buffalo. "To death," the guy replied. War Memorial Stadium was an eerie place to play. Security guards and riot police wearing helmets and carrying clubs were everywhere to protect the players from the fans and the fans from each other. The people carry shopping bags full of beer and sandwiches and thermos bottles filled with spirits. The dressing room was on the second floor, and we had to walk about 100 yards under the stadium to the field. A chicken-wire restraining fence was all that separated us from the belligerent Buffalo fans. I was just thankful that this would be the last game in that place. The Bills would move into a new, 80,000-seat stadium in suburban Orchard Park for the '73 season.

Once again there was a thirty-five-mile-an-hour crosswind to screw up Plunkett's passing, and the effect was even more disastrous on the punting game. ("How," asked Studstill, "are you supposed to kick when you're blown flat on your back?") And Carl Garrett's knee was bothering him again, and we were losing passes and punts in the sun, but there was really no excuse. (Even though on the flight back to Boston it seemed as if everybody on the team, myself included, had one to offer.) The Bills just stomped us silly, 38-14, on a day we couldn't do anything right.

But the next game was back in Schaefer against the Jets, and we had a two-game winning streak going at home. We practiced all week on shutting off Joe Namath and his aerial attack.

So, naturally, Namath only threw eight passes the entire game. Meanwhile, John Riggins and Emerson Boozer combined for over 100 yards rushing apiece and the team wound up with a 396 yard total offense. Defensive coach Dick Evans flashed hand signals all afternoon and in exasperation finally started screaming instructions to Cheyunski. Nothing worked. Eventually, Chey started ignoring Evans and called his own defenses. They weren't any more effective, but then I suppose they weren't any worse either.

The Jets just did whatever they wanted to with us. It was mayhem. After they'd trounced us 41-13 we were shell-shocked in the locker room. And now we had two tough road games ahead of us.

The whole atmosphere was becoming unbearably strained

around Foxboro. The offense had been sputtering. Plunkett hadn't thrown well since the Redskin game, and we had surrendered seventy-nine points to the opposition in the past two games. To top it all off, Carl Garrett was nowhere to be found; he didn't show for practice once all week. Nothing was said on the matter by the coaching staff, but the locker room scuttlebutt abounded with absurd rumors. Over the course of the week I heard that: (a) Garrett had been traded, (b) Garrett had been suspended, (c) Garrett had retired. I even heard that Garrett had been forcibly inducted into the army. A story was that he was in the reserves and was not regarded as exactly a model soldier.

When we boarded the plane for Pittsburgh Carl Garrett was surprisingly present, and although Bob Gladieux had worked out with the first team all week, no one doubted that Garrett would get the nod the next day. He was two thirds of our offense, and the way things had been going for Jim, Carl was virtually indispensable.

*

The whole weekend was a bummer, one of the worst of my life. Somebody screwed up and there were no buses waiting for us at the Pittsburgh airport. We were dropped at an obscure air-freight hangar a mile from the terminal, where we waited in the cold for over an hour, shivering in a drizzle before our transportation arrived.

Then, Spiro Agnew was in town that night to give a campaign speech at our hotel and the place was crawling with furtive Secret Service agents and inebriated Republicans. Rather than wait for an elevator for the privilege of riding with a bunch of obnoxious drunks, I made the mistake of walking down two flights of stairs, using the back stairway. The doors locked behind me; I was trapped in the fire exit.

I had to walk, sweating, snarling, and cursing all the way, down twenty-four flights of stairs to the street level, and when I opened the door a siren went off and I was suddenly surrounded by about twenty cops and Secret Service agents. I was scared to death. I finally convinced them I wasn't the incarnation of Lee Harvey Oswald and they let me go. I should have kept my mouth shut and let them take me away.

The game was an utter nightmare. The Steelers' notorious front four made mincemeat out of Plunkett. Mean Joe Greene and company sacked him six times and brutally manhandled him all afternoon. We were totally outclassed; at one point we had the ball in a third down and fifty-five situation. Franco's Italian Army, Gerela's Gorillas, and Ham's Polacks all had a field day as Pittsburgh tore us apart, 33-3.

The plane trip home was an experience in pathos. I sat with a battered, bruised, and beaten Jim Plunkett. His passing statistics were atrocious, and he had taken one of the worst physical beatings a quarterback has ever undergone that day. Still, he was inwardly questioning himself and shouldering the blame for our collapse in his own mind. Jim just couldn't admit that it was impossible to throw the football while lying dormant on the ground. He was badly beaten up; his eye and lip were swollen. He looked kind of like Carmen Basilio after one of his fights with Sugar Ray Robinson. I felt true compassion for the kid. He was a winner and couldn't comprehend why we were getting clobbered week in and week out.

Worse yet, morale and pride had so ebbed that several of the players were cutting up, joking and laughing just as if we'd won. We'd not only lost, we'd been thoroughly embarrassed and humiliated, and, it seemed, some players didn't really give a damn anymore.

Mazur sat alone in the front of the plane, silently staring out the window. Occasionally he would glance back in despair to where all the gleeful noise was emanating from. It was sad. The evening sky outside the jet seemed even darker, and the lights of Boston below never looked so good to me. At least we could forget about the embarrassment down at Daisy Buchanan's. Alcohol has a way of assuaging gloom.

⁕

Plunkett quietly contemplated his drink at a corner table that night, staring at the glass through the one eye that wasn't swollen shut. He hurt too much to move. Or even stand up.

"Don't worry," someone tried to console him, "it isn't you. It's the fucking Patriots. It's always been like this."

"You know something?" Jim looked up. "That's what they used to tell me in college. We'd get beat and people would say, 'It isn't you; it's just Stanford.' I decided that I was going to be the guy to change all that. And I did. And that's what I was determined to do here. This team was going to turn all that around.

"Now." He quietly shook him head. "I'm not so sure anymore."

I was thinking that when a competitor like Plunkett is that down, we're all in big trouble. Things, I had a feeling, might get a lot worse before they began to get better.

*

Mazur was taking an awful rap from the press. Everyone knew the consequences: if he didn't perform a miracle and perform one quickly his career in New England was due to rapidly terminate. Practices began to assume an atmosphere of uncertainty and disorganization. The pressure was getting to everyone.

We traveled to New York and were summarily crushed by the Jets again. They seemingly could beat nobody but us, but they did that with ease. The game at Shea marked the first time in Jim Plunkett's entire career that he had been removed from a game for ineptitude. When he was six for twenty-seven with three interceptions, Mazur pulled him in favor of Brian Dowling.

In 1971 every loss was regarded as sort of a laboratory lesson in pro football. Plunkett had played every down on offense, and our record for the last half of the season had improved to 4-3. This year the desperation had reached such proportions that now Jim was being yanked for Dowling, a signal caller with little experience.

The atmosphere everywhere on the team was by now desperation city. Everybody was looking for excuses. It was Mazur's fault. It was Bell's fault. It was Plunkett's fault. The offense. The defense. Everybody but our own damn selves. We were, just like in 1970, thinking like losers.

*

And the local media castrated us. Barely a month earlier we had been "the best young team in football." Now there were headlines like "Is Football the Patriots Game?" TV sportscaster Clark Booth suggested that we gave the word ineptitude a bad name. And, since our next game was a Monday night ABC telecast against the 1-6 Colts, there was all sorts of cruel speculation about what the network could possibly do to retain the audience, much less get people to tune in in the first place. Poor Howard!

And the press was getting to some of the players. Two-hundred-fifty-pound defensive end Dennis Wirgowski obscenely expressed a desire to throttle Boston *Globe* columnist Jack Craig. Craig had written that Wirgowski's playing an entire game on the line suggested that Bell had provided Mazur scant talent to work with.

Eddie Andelman, the radio talk show moderator, was on Mike Montler's shit list too. Montler publicly stated that he wanted to meet Andelman with the express purpose of knocking his teeth out. A lot of the guys had stopped reading the newspapers altogether.

While we didn't exactly redeem ourselves against the Colts, we played our best game in weeks, losing 24-17 with both teams playing much better than the records going into the game would have led one to expect. But the whole contest was marred by the fan reaction. They were now thoroughly down on us.

It was actually quite ugly. Coming out of the passageway leading to the field we were greeted with a barrage of beer, obscenities, and insults. During the game they were throwing whiskey bottles onto the field, and the signs and banners hung around the stadium reflected the climate. In full view for the national TV audience were, among others, "Send Upton Uptown," "Bell-Mazur—The Gruesome Twosome," and "Sullivan's Foxboro Follies — Rated X."

When the game ended the fans were literally spitting at us. One drunk challenged Mike Montler to a fight. The guy didn't know that Mike had buried his father two days earlier, and Mike snapped. He went crazy. He hurled his helmet at the guy and charged after him. It took three players to restrain him from going right over the wall after the idiot. Had he gotten his hands on him he would have, without question, been charged with manslaughter.

＊

Mazur was thoroughly wrung out. He looked terrible. He had taken to spending nights on a couch in his office after staying up until the wee hours trying to figure out some way to pull the team together. The once well built Notre Dame quarterback was an emaciated figure; he'd lost thirty pounds during the '72 season. I really felt bad and not a little guilty to see him falling apart before my eyes. To make matters worse, all he had staring him in the face was a trip to Miami to play the undefeated Dolphins.

＊

Before we left the hotel for the Orange Bowl I remember sitting beside the ocean and watching the surf roll in. There was something oddly incongruous about the serenity of it all. The calm before the storm.

Somewhere, sometime, someplace, some team must have

been beaten worse, but I've never heard of it. By half time we were behind 38-0, and the sole instruction we received between halves was very terse and to the point: "Defend yourselves as best you can." The Dolphins fans had produced their white handkerchiefs midway through the first period, and by the time the gun sounded its merciful coup de grâce we had been annihilated, 52-0. The Dolphins had celebrated Don Shula's hundredth victory by rolling up nearly 500 yards in total offense. It was the worst defeat, by far, in our history, and as Coach Mazur and Billy Sullivan occupied adjoining seats on the plane home, we were all aware that something had to happen.

It did. When I arrived at Schaefer for Tuesday's practice there was an unusual amount of commotion inside the offices. Reporters were scurrying about like so many mice. Time for the team meeting passed and no coaches showed up. It was strange. Finally Bell descended the stairs and told us what had happened. John Mazur had resigned. He'd had his fill of the Patriots' Revolution. Bell explained that Mazur "did a good job, but had resigned in the best interests of the club." He also informed us that an interim coach would be named within twelve hours and told us to go home. There would be no movies, practice, or meetings.

Several of us assembled in shock and sadness at the nearby Red Snapper. It was like a wake. We were speaking in near whispers. We felt we'd let the man down. He couldn't block and tackle for us. Mazur had been a gentleman who enjoyed a laugh, a fifteen-cent cigar, and a cold beer now and then, and even players who questioned his coaching methods felt rotten to see him go this way.

So, the reasoning went, Bell would finally bring in his new head coach next year. He'd finally gotten his wish, and we could, we assumed, be playing for an Arnsbarger or a Schellenberger the next season. We were also speculating on the identity of the mysterious "interim coach." Offensive coordinator Sam Rutigliano would have seemed to be the logical choice, but he quickly quashed *that* speculation. "The interim coaching job isn't a position," said Sam correctly, "it's a sentence."

On Wednesday Bell announced the appointment of Phil Bengtson to the interim spot. The former Packer coach, once Vince Lombardi's top assistant, had been borrowed from the Chargers for the balance of the season. His presence did stimulate some semblance of renewed pride, a sense of belonging, but he was also somewhat enigmatic. When one reporter asked him, for instance, his impression of the team, he replied that we were "good-looking boys." He made it clear from the start that the younger players would get a shot at playing regularly. He wanted to look at everybody. Several veterans who'd been playing regularly suddenly found themselves riding the bench. But at least the practices were easier.

Things improved around Foxboro, but we kept losing. Buffalo and Baltimore whacked us for losses number seven and eight in a row, and then the Dolphins came to town. We actually played our best game in the two months we hadn't won, and the 37-21 score was thirty-six points better than we'd fared against them the last time around.

When we showed up on Tuesday it was déjà vu: mysterious activity in the offices, strange reporters bustling about.

Then another bombshell burst. Three weeks after he had attained his two-year objective and rid himself of John Mazur, Upton Bell had gotten the sack himself. Presumably again "for the good of the team," Billy Sullivan had shit-canned the boy wonder. Jesus Christ, we were thinking, next thing you know he's going to fire himself!

We flew to New Orleans for another battle of the also-rans. We were now 2-10; the Saints were 2-9-1. We hit the French Quarter with a vengeance that night. It was one giant drunken brawl of a party. Players were invading strip joints, hanging from lampposts, staggering and crawling around Bourbon Street like an army just about to march into a big battle.

Who the hell could blame us for drowning our sorrows and apprehensions? In the past nine weeks we had lost all our games, our head coach, and our general manager; our quarterback was suffering through a miserable season and was such a basket case he could barely walk, and Bengtson was evaluating our performance to see who was worth retaining for another season. A mint julep, I'll tell you, never tasted so good.

When we took the field for what had been billed as a showdown between the two young superstar quarterbacks, Plunkett and Archie Manning, we were startled to hear the unfamiliar sound of cheers. It seemed that New Orleans fans were up in arms, demanding the resignation of *their* coach, J. D. Roberts, but in the case of the Saints there was an additional complication. Roberts happened to be related by marriage to Saints owner John Mecom.

But the backing of the crowd seemed to give us a much-needed lift, and we responded by winning for the first time in over two months by a score of 17-10. We assured ourselves, thereby, of losing the distinction of being the worst team in pro football and let the number one draft choice slip away to the Houston Oilers. And it was almost comforting to watch the New Orleans fans serenade the coach with a chorus of "Goodbye, J.D., it's great to see you go." I realized that at least we weren't the only screwed-up franchise in the NFL.

＊

We went through the last week of practice with mixed emotions. We were, naturally, all relieved to see the fiasco of a season come to an end, but there was also a pervasive sense of sadness, as many of us realized that we wouldn't be around again for another year in New England. With Upton Bell gone, there were bound to be wholesale shakeups in personnel, and there was always the nagging specter of the mysterious "Bengtson Report."

The last week of practice is traditionally treated as a joke. You go through the motions, meetings are cut to a bare minimum, and the game plan is simplified to just a few plays. In the locker room many of the guys steal everything in sight: sweatshirts, socks, jocks, and even toilet articles. Equipment manager George Luongo estimates that $1000 worth of booty disappears the last week each season.

＊

Fittingly enough for me, the final game of the season was in Denver. It was a nostalgic occasion for me personally.

That first year we'd been 3-11, and here I was coming back with a team that was 3-10. I also sensed that this might well be my last game as a Patriot and possibly my last in professional football. The era of the good-blocking, slow-moving tight end was on the wane. Players of my ilk, like Fred Arbanas and Pete Lammons, were going the way of the passenger pigeon in favor of speed burners like Charlie Sanders and Riley Odoms. In five short years the game had changed, subtly but dramatically.

The game differed little from ten others we'd played that year. My old teammates played well in taking my current ones to the cleaners, and the final was 45-21. Bengtson told us afterward in the visitors' locker room that we'd done a good job in just hanging together. We had, he told us, given it the best we could, but our talent was limited. "No shit," I was thinking. But the omen was clear. Wholesale changes were in order. Bengtson had been hired to keep us together for five weeks, which he had done, and to diagnose the symptoms of whatever fatal disease afflicted us, which, we knew, he would do. Scrupulously. It didn't bode well for many people.

The coaches made the rounds, shaking hands and wishing everyone a Merry Christmas. There was no talk of "See you next year" or "Keep in shape."

They knew their fates and we knew ours. There was no tomorrow for them in Foxboro; they could expect to be unemployed within a month or so.

As I pulled off my mud-caked uniform I reminisced with my friend Ron Berger. Everything had started off so optimistically in the summer. Winner, shit! The dream had become a nightmare.

But there's one thing about professional football players: They're realists, and I instinctively suspected, as did Ron, that my days as a New England Patriot might very well have come to an end.

The Coming
of the Messiah

No sooner had our '72 season ended than speculation began regarding the identity of the new head coach. Literally dozens of names were bandied about, and for every name there were a dozen rumors. We all knew that many of our teammates, some of them very close friends, wouldn't be back the next year. Hell, none of us could be sure we'd be back ourselves. There were even rumors that the Patriots were considering trading Plunk for roughly half a football team.

The apprehension inspired by the prospect of uprooting a family and moving cross-country — or worse, having a career swiftly and prematurely curtailed — tends to make a football player's stomach queasy. After all, when a new coach arrives on the scene he is wont, more often than not, to harbor a disdain for players from his predecessor's regime. I suppose the rationale holds that the incumbent players lost for the other coach, so the new man can't do anything worse than lose with his own players. In any case, we were

John Mazur's players, and John Mazur had resigned under, to put it mildly, duress. Ergo, it seemed reasonable to expect that the new head man — when they got one — would arrive at Schaefer Stadium, rid himself of Mazur's losing staff and losing players, and begin anew.

I could see the writing on the wall. I'd been through it all before on the other end of the stick six years before as a rookie when Lou Saban came into Denver and literally swept the locker room clean of the old Broncos and their losing ways. Unfortunately, it has yet to be demonstrated that wholesale purges of players rid a losing team of its inherent cancer. A better case can be made for the syndrome starting at the top. Anyway, we said our fond farewells and wished each other luck.

Many of the players were extremely apprehensive, indeed skeptical, about interim coach Phil Bengtson. Some vehemently objected to him and his comparatively traditional methods. Mike Montler, for instance, insisted that he'd never return to "this sick team. The whole organization stinks," said Mike. "I'll retire before I'll come back here."

While Mike was just one of many who were unhappy in New England, I could tell from the look in his eyes that he, for one, was not kidding. I sat on the plane talking with my old roomie Jack Maitland, who was probably more relieved than anyone that it was all over and done with. He'd confided in me a month earlier that he was fed up with football. After three years in the NFL he'd gone from a Super Bowl ring with the Colts to playing on the Patriots special teams, and he'd acquired a case of very shot nerves. "Christ," Jack told me, "this last month was pure hell. All I could think of was getting a knee torn up on a punt or a kick-off."

When you're thinking like that, you *know* it's time to quit, pension or no pension. Besides, Jack's family had enough money to make the decision easier for him than for another guy.

Most of us thought Bengtson's major accomplishments had come in avoiding a full-scale mutiny by the players and keeping the fans from ripping our collective jugular veins. We'd won one game (over the equally dismal New Orleans Saints) and lost four under his direction, but what weighed more importantly on everyone's mind was the intriguing Bengtson Report he was compiling.

When Mazur had "resigned" on the plane coming back from Miami, Bell had come up with the "interim coach" concept. Laboring under the delusion that he'd be around to pick a new head coach (as things turned out, Bell's stay in Foxboro outlasted Mazur's by less than a month), Upton had obtained Bengtson "on loan" from his administrative job with the Chargers (it developed during the '74 draft that the transaction had cost the Pats a third-round pick — and Bengtson never did return to San Diego) with instructions to compile a comprehensive dossier on the team for the edification of the new head coach, whoever he might be. Initially we shuddered at the prospect. Hell, in the first place, why *should* Bengtson give anybody a good evaluation? He was supposed to be going back to San Diego. Besides, he'd come on the scene at the tail end of a very demoralized year when hardly any of us were playing at 100 percent efficiency — mentally or, certainly, physically. Most of us were playing hurt. How are you supposed to judge a beauty contest when all the girls are wrapped up in bandages?

Eventually the attitude mellowed into "What's going to happen is going to happen," and we even began to joke philosophically about the Bengtson Report. "I *know* I'm going to get a low rating," said Rick Cash. "Bengtson's the guy who traded me from Green Bay."

Jim Cheyunski, our starting middle linebacker for the past four years, was despondent over the fact that Bengtson had benched him in favor of rookie Ralph Cindrich. "I guess he doesn't like one-legged Polacks," muttered Jim. The Bengtson Report got more ink in Boston than the Pentagon Papers. Every reporter in town would've given his typewriter, his left testicle, and a player to be named later to sneak a look at it.

*

As the weeks slowly passed the list of coaches declining to accept the Patriots job kept growing. Joe Paterno of Penn State was supposedly signed, sealed, and delivered. The local media reported that Billy Sullivan had made him an offer he couldn't refuse. I don't know where the information came from, but it obviously wasn't from Paterno, because the next day he respectfully announced that he was not about to leave his secure job at Penn State for the circus in Foxboro.

Other names cropped up and vanished from sight with equal alacrity. Darrell Royal of Texas. Bob Devaney of Nebraska. John McKay of U.S.C. Duffy Daugherty of Michigan State. All said, "Thanks, but no thanks." It had become abundantly clear that just as no one wanted the job, the Patriots people definitely were on the prowl for a coach from the collegiate ranks. Earlier speculation had elicited a few names associated with professional football: Ernie Stautner and Howard Schnellenberger. For all I know they might've turned the Patriots down too, but in any case as the weeks passed all we heard about were college coaches. Ara Parseghian? Bear Bryant? No way. People were getting frantic because with the college draft less than a week away New England had no coach and no general manager.

They finally struck pay dirt on Friday, January 26, exactly four days before the draft was scheduled to commence, when they named Oklahoma head coach Chuck Fairbanks to the dual position of coach and general manager.

Late that day I received a phone call from Bill Kipouras of the *Herald-American*. He had learned from someone that Fairbanks had been an assistant at Houston when I played there and wanted to sound out my impressions.

For the first time in my career I ducked it. I lied. I genuinely feared for my job, and I was well aware that straightforward answers to Kip's questions might have me packing before Fairbanks drafted a player. I could have kicked myself in the ass. "You can't sweet-talk your way into a job," I told myself. I knew I was finished in Boston. Between Fairbanks, the Bengtson Report, and the umpteenth new era everyone was talking about, it looked nothing short of hopeless from my end.

But while I was fully cognizant of all this, Kipouras' story the next day had me quoted saying things like "Chuck is a very dynamic, hardworking young man. He gets the maximum out of his players. He's dedicated, was well-liked, and is definitely a motivator."

I couldn't find enough glowing adjectives in my vocabulary when I described him on the telephone. I gave him credit for developing the wishbone offense. I said he'd revolutionized college football. Thank God I had the countenance, at least, not to predict a Super Bowl victory in 1973. I seem to recall that was on the tip of my tongue.

I had copped out, though. I knew Fairbanks was anything but a superman. As a matter of fact, far from being a source of inspiration to players, he seemed to avoid them, intentionally keeping his distance.

In 1971 I had briefly roomed with Steve Casteel, who'd played linebacker for Fairbanks at Oklahoma. Just before lights out, Steve would tell some horror stories about Fairbanks' training regimentation at O.U. All I could think of at the time was "Thank Christ he wasn't the *head* coach at Houston." And now here he was the chief honcho in New England.

The night before Kipouras' article appeared, several of my teammates had called to inquire about the new coach. I leveled with them. I didn't want to lie to them too. They, at least, deserved to know their fate. I remember I kept saying to myself as I hung up, "Don't worry about the new coach, fellas. We won't be around long enough to get to know him very well."

*

Three days later the Patriots held their draft. Fairbanks'

first move as head coach was to trade the team's best all-around player, Carl Garrett, to Chicago for a number one choice. To me Carl Garrett had been the incarnation of Gale Sayers. He could, very simply, do it all. He possessed an uncanny instinct for running with a football. Garrett could sense an oncoming tackler, put a move on him, and be right past him in a split second. The guy could cut on a dime and dart through a hole the size of a pea. Besides his ability in the running department, he had great hands and was a fantastic kick return specialist. He also was one tough son of a bitch on the field. I suppose you could say his only real weakness was off the field. Carl was single, drove a Corvette, and loved the ladies. This, combined with a general dislike for practice, undoubtedly put him at the top of the blacklist via the Bengtson Report, although I personally think he'd have been brought into line by the proper discipline. He might have missed a few practices, but there was no question about desire; Carl Garrett frequently played hurt.

The following day Leigh Montville, a likable sportswriter who covers the Pats for the Boston *Globe*, had a story about the Garrett trade on page one of the sports section. He'd discussed it with Montler and Cheyunski, whose reactions appeared in black and white. "You can quote me," Mike had told him. "I think this is really a pretty good trade, probably just as good as the Nick Buoniconti trade and all those other successful trades this team has made."

He was referring to the 1969 trade that sent the All-Pro middle linebacker to the Miami Dolphins for journeyman linebacker Bull Bramlett and third-string quarterback Kim

Hammond. Buoniconti went on to lead Miami's famous "No Name Defense" and has played in the last three Super Bowls. Bramlett lasted two years with the Pats before being traded for someone named "Man Mountain" Moore, who never made the team. Hammond hung around for a year on the taxi squad before deciding that he was more suited to law school than to professional football.

"We just traded away the best player on our team," Montler continued. "Jim Plunkett included. This trade staggers me. It hurts me to read a word like 'controversial' in front of Carl's name, like he was Duane Thomas or something. He wasn't."

I knew Mike wanted to be traded. After reading the article I also knew his wish would be granted. "Needless to say, I was surprised that we shored up our offense so much," he added. "That's great. Now we'll score thirty-five points and lose by two."

Cheyunski's attitude was slightly less outspoken, but no less emphatic. "Maybe they're trying to build the team with draft choices, but I guess I'm like George Allen. I can't see trading a proven veteran for a draft choice. Carl was ninety percent of our offense last year. I hate to see him go. It feels good when you're playing hard to look up and see someone else who's doing it too."

Cheyunski, ever the realist, also knew where his destiny lay. "I'll be busy. I just had an operation on my hand, my wife had a baby, and we just bought a new house in Plymouth. I'll have a lot to do, all this, plus waiting for the trade lists."

Goodbye, Mike, I was thinking. Goodbye, Jim. I just

hope you go anywhere but Houston. You deserve better than that.

In mid-February the 1776 Club, a group of boosters, tossed its annual Patriots fete at the Sidney Hill Country Club. It provided Fairbanks with an opportunity to show off his top four draft choices, presumably offering hope for the future. It wasn't the most comfortable place to be a veteran; there isn't much satisfaction to be gained in extolling the virtues of some guy who's been hired to take your place.

Jim Cheyunski was in attendance, sporting a full growth of facial hair, a beautiful red beard. I asked him about the *Globe* story. He said that he didn't much give a damn about anything. He just voiced his inner feelings. I had to admire his attitude.

The new coaches went around introducing themselves at the banquet. The only one of Fairbanks' new staff I hadn't yet met was Bill Pace, the offensive backfield coach. A former head coach at Vanderbilt, Pace was to resign a week later — fully six months before the Pats first exhibition game — to become offensive backfield coach under Billy Fulcher at Georgia Tech! Very interesting, I thought. Maybe Pace was the smartest of the lot of them.

The evening consisted of the usual several dozen speeches, promises, and hopes for the future. Veterans made small talk with the draftees, albeit through a lot of forced smiles, and Fairbanks even danced with the wife of number one draft pick John Hannah. The 1776 Club people were mumbling about how excited they were about the coming season. It was all a masquerade. The 1776 Club dinner was clearly, to most of us, the lull before the storm.

The first warnings were evinced shortly. We were each sent a letter "inviting" us to a March "orientation camp" in Tampa, the first ever for a Patriot team. It was allegedly "voluntary," but when we received our plane tickets in the mail from business manager Herman Bruce, unasked-for, a few days later it was pretty clear just how voluntary it was. At first glance, four days in the sun appeared to be a welcome respite from the cold and wind of Boston in early March.

About ten of us flew on the same flight from Boston that Friday morning, each apprehensive to one degree or another about our futures with the team. I, for one, was convinced that my chances of staying with the Patriots were minimal. At any rate, some proceeded to drink themselves into a state of paralysis on the free booze in the first-class section. What could they do to us when we got to Tampa, anyway, we were asking — put us in a meat grinder?

I was close. We landed and took the hotel limousine to the Hawaiian Village, a pseudoexotic motel across the highway from the Cincinnati Reds spring training headquarters.

We had a meeting called for six o'clock that evening. Coach Fairbanks formally introduced himself and his coaching staff to the squad. It seemed as if there were more coaches than players — seven or eight assistants, a strength coach, a flexibility coach. A year or two before the trainer had had to stage open warfare to get an assistant, and now there were so many coaches they got in each other's way. I assumed that Fairbanks must've had a new budget allocated.

We were each handed a thick booklet detailing the weekend's activities. The cover was black. Foreboding, I thought. The first page was a mimeographed form letter from "The Coach":

Gentlemen:
This is the beginning of a new era for you and I [sic]
and the New England Patriots . . .

Indeed.

Then he talked about class. He had, he informed us, surrounded himself with a class coaching staff and wanted players with class as well. The era of the big dumb jock was a thing of the past, we were told. He then proceeded to rip into several players who had been observed winging beer bottles from the motel balcony into the swimming pool fifty yards away. Within two months two of them were traded.

We were then asked to return to our rooms to review the booklets and instructed to follow the itinerary to the second — no time would be wasted. Some of us did. Others repaired to various saloons in the neighborhood; in his infinite wisdom, Fairbanks had located us in a plush motel right in the midst of the hooker section of Tampa.

We were aroused at 7:00 A.M. every morning that weekend and bused to a local high school, remaining at the prescribed workout site until 5:00 P.M. each evening. It seemed like the late-July two-a-days were already at hand; we were even issued helmets. Each minute was spent exploring every new technique and learning all the new terminology imaginable. (During the passing drills, a defensive back picked off one errant toss and a coach came jogging onto the field. "Wait a minute," he said, "what was the interception call last year?" *Fire!*" replied an ambitious second-year secondary player. "Well, let's change it!" the coach retorted.

Following the hour-and-a-half morning workouts, we were treated to a catered lunch: dry sandwiches, cookies, and apples. Most of us were too tired to eat. After a forty-five-minute lunch break we had an afternoon program of lectures, meetings, and another practice session to look forward to. Holiday, my ass. We were longing for the comparative tranquillity of a Boston snowstorm. It was pure hell, because, caught on such short notice — and having so little notion of what to anticipate — most players were in relatively poor condition.

Ralph Cindrich twisted a knee. Then Denny Wirgowski pulled a hamstring. Then it was my turn. Running on unsteady legs, I completely tore the cartilage in my right knee — the same one that had been injured during the '72 season. I had the distinction of being the first player in the history of the NFL to undergo surgery for a spring training injury.

Following the Monday practice session we were allowed to return home, with one small formality. Just before checkout time the festivities were topped off with a twelve-minute run, with everyone expected to make at least a mile and a half during the allotted time. Fewer than half the players did.

The players limped home. Nobody had ever expected the Tampa spring camp to be a veritable buzz saw. The linemen hit without pads. Drills were long and tiresome. And the screaming. The new staff took little time in laying down the law of the land. If somebody screwed up they were met with a verbal barrage. Grown men were being humiliated much to the amusement of the gawking public, who watched practice every day in the eighty-five-degree temperatures.

Upon arriving in Boston I had my right knee operated on, thanks to the spring camp. I was now faced with the monumental task of rehabilitating a knee in only three months' time.

Fairbanks had another weekend training session in May. This time, however, the players met at nearby Schaefer Stadium. They were tested to see how much progress they had achieved since the Tampa horror show. The majority of the veterans showed up in relatively good shape. This time the players were treated to shoulder pads along with their helmets. The linemen hit, the backs hit. Everybody hit except the quarterbacks and kickers. The veterans were pissed, but what could they do? Everyone was fighting for his life.

While I watched the insanity from the sanctity of the end zone, I thought of Mazur's relaxed spring camp about this time last year. What a difference a year makes.

The screaming and shouting was laughable. The hitting despicable. It was a bona-fide zoo and I was limping around the field on a gimpy knee. I was inwardly happy though. At least I was spared the aggravation of going through this pure unadulterated horseshit!

Driving to the summer training site at Amherst gave me time to think. My knee was close to 100 percent. Thanks to long hours of rehabilitation, I was in great shape and resolved to give everything to make the team. Football was my life and Fairbanks' Gestapo-like camp wasn't going to come between us. He said every player would be given an equal chance to make his ball club. Fair enough, I thought.

I never was more wrong.

✻

We assembled for pictures, and this was followed by the now fabled twelve-minute run. I sensed from the beginning of the day that I was on my way out. In past years I'd been included in several different photo poses — with the receivers, action shots, head shots, in both color and in black and white. This day, however, no pictures of me were taken. I was seated in the midst of a dozen free agents who had no chance of making the ball club, watching the proceeding. My stock was beginning to tumble rapidly. Then came the marathon — the twelve-minute run. Twelve minutes can seem like an hour. The tight ends — in this case, Bob Windsor and myself — had to run with the greyhounds, the wide receivers, Randy Vataha and his crew of sprinters.

The horn sounded and everyone took off. I stayed right behind Randy for the entire first lap. Then I passed him and led for the second. My teammates were cheering me on from the sidelines, and it felt good to know that someone was actually rooting you on. My leading Vataha was not unakin to Mr. Ed setting a pace for Secretariat. It was just a matter of time before he would overtake me; I knew that.

But I felt good, and I was setting an excellent pace. Randy caught me at the beginning of the third lap. Then Reggie Rucker passed me as well and I was running third. I caught a glimpse of Fairbanks watching the proceedings with an intent look on his face. Just before we hit the fourth lap I was surprised to find myself lapping Windsor, our starting tight end. That, I confess, gave me extra incentive. I wanted to prove to Fairbanks that I'd trained exactly as he'd told me to. I'd come back from knee surgery in barely three months, after all, and here I was beating most of the wide receivers and finishing first among the tight ends.

When the ordeal ended I'd held up for third. I'd also finished a lap and a half ahead of Windsor. Despite the pain, I felt exhilarated. The hard work I'd done all spring had paid off. Those long hours of lifting weights and running had prepared me for the fight.

*

There were over 100 players on the field for the first day of camp that summer in Amherst. The lines for drills were half a field long. There were so many bodies that they got in one another's way.

I noticed that I was listed as the number three tight end on the depth chart. Windsor was first, and Bob Adams, a former Pittsburgh Steeler obtained in an off-season trade, was listed second. Word also had it that Bucko Kilroy was high on a rookie from Maryland named Don Ratliff. Ratliff was a converted defensive end, and I suppose Kilroy was still determined to find that diamond in the rough.

A friend in the front office had also told me that Sam Rutigliano was touting a free agent rookie named Jerry Broadneaux. Sam, John Mazur's offensive coordinator, had been the sole holdover retained by the Fairbanks regime.

Everything was filmed. Simple passing drills, blocking exercises, even calisthenics were committed to celluloid. With the lines the size they were, a player was lucky if he had one opportunity to catch a ball. Fairbanks, meanwhile, rode through camp in a golf cart, sort of like General Patton. He was carrying a long stick. I'd had a colonel in the army who carried a swagger stick. He rode around in a jeep and would periodically stop to scream at some weary recruit. At least he admitted to wanting to *be* like General Patton.

The second day of workouts began with the sun shining through the Venetian blinds of my room in fly-infested Emerson House, our latest summer quarters. (Fairbanks had moved us out of the UMass dorm we'd used in previous years.)

I was laid out on the bed, collecting my thoughts. During two-a-days, players have a tendency to lose all conception of time and place. I remember I'd just flipped on the radio and heard that the Red Sox had lost the night before and that the weather would be hot and humid — high in the mid-nineties — and that I was already worrying about the heat that afternoon when I heard a knock on the door.

It was a rather cold, imperious knock, and I remember the thought flashing to mind that I'd been traded. I dismissed that notion immediately. Impossible, I thought. Cut? Not a chance. I've only been here a day, and besides, Fairbanks has already gone on record as saying he'd give everyone a fair shot, an equal chance to make the team.

I opened the door. It was a total stranger, a pimply-faced kid, the assistant to the assistant jockstrap washer. "Tom Beer. Coach Bengtson wants to see you at eight-thirty in room one fifteen." He turned and fled.

Son of a bitch, I thought. What the hell for? My mind was doing complete somersaults by then. I couldn't think straight. Then I remembered that I'd had some crazy dream the night before about getting the ax. I couldn't remember the details, but I could recall the cold, helpless feeling that had crept over my entire body, and I could feel it again in the morning. I started to get scared. I had a premonition that for the first time in my career I was about to meet The Turk.

At 8:25 I began a slow, deliberate walk downstairs to the basement where the brass had their offices and sleeping quarters. I reached Bengtson's room, paused a few seconds, and took a deep breath. I knocked on the door.

"Sit down, Tom," he told me. When I'd complied he went on.

"After evaluating the situation at tight end, we've decided to let you go. I know how hard you've worked this off season, and the reason we're letting you go early is to give you a chance to hook on with another club. Please check with Bucko Kilroy about your termination papers and your physical. Good luck.

"And, oh yes. Don't forget to bring me your playbook."

I was stunned. I couldn't begin to comprehend what he'd just said. There was a lump in my throat and I couldn't speak. I felt like a drowning man as my whole football career flashed through my mind. I was furious, sure, but I was also crushed. And, I felt, for the first time in my career, unwanted.

Now I knew why Fairbanks was so interested in my damn knee. The only thing he'd said to me before the start of Friday's practice had been to "make sure my knee was O.K." If my knee was O.K. there would be no basis for an injury grievance claim.

I dragged myself out of Bengtson's room and down the hall to Kilroy's office. Bucko had the pleasure of processing every player who was dropped from the team. I'd heard in the past through the grapevine that he didn't think too highly of me. I never placed much stock in that sort of rumor; all I knew was that every year he brought in a bunch of stiffs to take my place, and every year I beat them out.

He was waiting for me. "Will you please sign this paper releasing you from further employment with us. Sign that paper too." He pointed to the waiver procedure directive.

He had me sign a few more things. I'm not sure to this day what some of them were. "If you hurry," he said, "you can catch one of the doctors at the Student Health Center. You need to have a termination physical. Good luck." I could barely make out his speech. He had a big, fat cigar stuck in the corner of his mouth.

I didn't give him the pleasure of shaking my hand. You might say that we weren't parting on the friendliest of terms.

"Don't forget," he called as I walked out the door, "to give Coach Bengtson your playbook."

❋

When I left Kilroy's room I chanced upon Tom Boisture in the hallway. Boisture had been my high school coach back at St. Ambrose in Detroit. He'd moved to Houston as an assistant and recruited me down there. He was now a Patriots scout, working for Chuck Fairbanks.

I could tell he felt badly about what had happened. As we chatted briefly he assured me that someone would pick me up right away. Kind words from a true friend, I thought. I was embarrassed, because I could feel tears forming in my eyes. I tried to hold them back.

I'd played on two of Boisture's city and state championship teams in high school — the salad days. Now he was trying to console me. I suppose you could say the man had seen me through thick and thin. He wished me luck and then said, "Coach Fairbanks wants to see you. He's upstairs."

I'm an eternal optimist. I honestly thought maybe he wanted to make me a scout or something. Or perhaps he'd worked out a deal to place me with another team. I knocked on his door and entered.

"Tom," he began, "I'm going to give you an option of one of two things. You can either announce your retirement or go on waivers. We'll give you until Monday to make your decision. Good luck."

Son of a bitch, I thought. Thanks for the chance to visit for the weekend. I wheeled and started for the door with gritted teeth. "Don't forget to give your playbook to Coach Bengtson," he called after me.

✻

The doctor was waiting for me. He wasn't a bad guy. He apologized for not knowing anything about football and then asked how the Patriots were going to do that year.

"Shitty," I replied. He noticed that my blood pressure

was high. I explained to him that I'd just been cut by one of the worst teams in pro football. He nodded. I don't think he understood.

After I'd been pronounced fit to be placed on waivers, I went to my room and packed my suitcases. I didn't want to stick around and say goodbye. I took the long way home. I figured I could think better while negotiating the curves on pastoral Route 2 than flying down the Massachusetts Turnpike. And I desperately needed to think.

As I drove toward Boston I began to notice simple things: waterfalls that I'd driven right past before, green trees and flowers, people vacationing and camping by the roadside, having a peaceful time in the serenity of western New England.

And I'd been told to take a hike after one meaningless day of practice. I reached Boston and immediately purchased two six-packs of Michelob before I retreated to the solitude of my apartment.

I sat there thinking and drinking, feeling angry, dejected, afraid, and uncertain all at once. I went over the events of the morning again and again in my mind. It was all very simple, yet unfathomable. I'd gotten up to go to practice, and barely two minutes later I was unemployed. At least I didn't have a family to support.

The afternoon passed into evening and I kept seeing Fairbanks and Kilroy. Neither one of them could look me in the eye when they spoke to me.

I also thought about all those speeches Fairbanks had made when he'd taken over. "Keep your nose clean, show a lot of class, and do what you're told. Everyone will have a fair chance to make my ball club."

Horseshit. He had given me one goddamn day. My own self-confidence was on the wane. Fairbanks had cut me and kept the Don Ratliffs and the Ashley Bells, guys who, in my opinion, hadn't a prayer of making anybody's football team. He had, of course, taken the time to inform me that I could retire.

I stayed in my apartment, alone, all weekend. I had plenty of company in my memories of times just past and worries about the future. I just sat and thought for days. I even wrote a poem, a memorial to my confused and disillusioned state of mind.

> *It's an empty, sick feeling*
> *sitting around alone by myself*
> *waiting, hoping, praying,*
> *staring at the telephone,*
> *jumping at its jingle.*
> *My destiny is now uncertain,*
> *a mist descending upon the Berkshires,*
> *the fog at dawn off Nantucket.*
> *I wait, I think, I hope*
> *into the wee small hours of the morning.*
> *What else is there to do*
> *after tears have dried?*

12

A Fleeting Touch of Class—Dolphin Style

I DIDN'T CALL Fairbanks back to let him know my decision. The choices he'd proposed — retire or be put on waivers Monday morning — left a bad taste in my mouth. I only knew I wasn't about to retire. I was bitter; I was pissed off. Who the hell did he think he was, anyway? Dictating what a player should do with his life. Hell, I was thinking, he never was good enough to play pro ball himself.

The days passed slowly. I played golf every day and ran every evening at Boston College. Physically I felt ready to go, but mentally it was a different story. No one had called me except a few reporters looking for something to write about. Kipouras of the *Herald-American* had written a piece that read like sort of an epitaph for Mr. Nice Guy — namely, me. I hadn't burned any bridges behind me in interviews. After all, what would have been the use? Fairbanks had been hired for some astronomical amount of money. I was unemployed.

On Tuesday the phone rang. I'd just returned from a round of golf with my friend Jimmy Rondeau, and the jingle stirred my pulse for perhaps the twentieth time that week.

It was Peter Hadhazy, the Patriots assistant general manager. My inclination was to tell him to bug off and leave me alone, but I didn't. What the hell, I reasoned, *he* hadn't been responsible for my departure. I was polite enough.

"Congratulations, Tom," said Hadhazy. "You've just been picked up on waivers by the Miami Dolphins. Give Pat Peppler a call, would you?"

I was flabbergasted. When I'd gotten the ax I had methodically reviewed the rosters of every team in the NFL and figured that if anyone was going to pick me up, New Orleans was the most likely. They had a bunch of has-beens and misfits at tight end. But *Miami?* The reigning Super Bowl champs! I'd always admired the team, but as I thought about it I kept reminding myself that they weren't superhumans either. Hell, the Patriots had beaten them in 1970 and again in 1971. The Dolphins still put their jocks on one leg at a time.

I sat down to try and gather my thoughts. Jesus, I was reeling. Fifteen minutes ago I'd been an unemployed hacker on the golf course; now I was a member of the world champions. I felt like I'd just won the Massachusetts State Lottery. The dream of every professional player, after all, is to play in the Super Bowl. A Super Bowl ring means you're the best, and here I was in a position to play for the best.

I called Peppler, who welcomed me to the Dolphins. He also informed me that Shula was encountering some difficulties negotiating incumbent tight end Marv Fleming's contract. Also Jim Mandich was hurt and wasn't working out with the team. "This is a great opportunity for you, Tom. Come on down as soon as you can," he said. I assured him

I'd be on the earliest jet. He told me someone would pick me up at the airport and said goodbye. As soon as he'd hung up I booked a flight on an Eastern 727 and went out to celebrate with my friends.

It was strange, but after I was cut by the Patriots you could have counted the number of friends who called or stopped by to see if I was O.K. on one hand. As soon as the news got out that I was a Dolphin though, the damn phone almost rang itself off the hook. So much for friends.

*

I flew first class to Miami, figuring that if I was going to be playing for a first-class organization I might as well begin by traveling first class. Questions kept running through my mind. What was Shula like? Were practices hard? What about the heat in Miami? I finally shut them all out of my thoughts. Who cared? I was a Dolphin, and that's all that really mattered to me. I was elated to realize that after the nightmares I'd undergone in Fairbanks' regime I was going to be associated with the best football team in the world.

I was greeted at the airport by a young fellow wearing a Banlon Dolphin shirt and chauffeured in the team limousine directly to the team doctor's for a physical. Everyone was very friendly, and I could tell that everyone from the nurses to the lab technicians were Dolphin fans. They talked about the team constantly. After the usual preliminaries — blood sample, pulse, and heartbeat — I was ushered into the doctor's lavish office. Herbert Virgin was the M.D.'s name, and you could tell from the contents of his wall that, unlike some team physicians I've encountered, the man was extremely successful in his practice. His wall was decorated with all sorts of degrees and awards from various schools and organizations.

I also noticed that Dr. Virgin was wearing his Super Bowl ring. It was beautiful. That ring, I was thinking, represents the pinnacle of what players slave and work their asses off for and never come close to getting. Hell, everyone connected with the team had a Super Bowl ring! I'd toiled for six years already without so much as a winning season, and here the guys who wash Manny Fernandez's jock all year get rings. I laughed to myself. More power to the lucky stiffs, I thought. This year I'll have one too.

＊

Virgin asked me about my medical background. I dictated my history of surgery and other assorted ailments into a recording device. I didn't resent it. His job was to make sure the Dolphins weren't about to sign a turkey. I asked him about Don Shula, and he replied that in Florida Shula was regarded as more than a football genius; he was God.

After Virgin had checked me out, I was herded into a room where the nurse took a few more tests. She, too, was a football fan, and at one point she asked me what position I played.

"Tight end," I replied.

"Oh." She smiled. "That's nice. We had another tight end taking his physical here today."

"Who?" I asked.

"Marv Fleming."

Son of a bitch. My excitement and exuberance tumbled as the bottom fell out of my heart. That, I was thinking, was a goddamn short holdout. Now instead of wondering about my new team I was wondering when the Dolphins were going to send me home.

Shula has a reputation around the league for sticking with his proven veterans. Only the exceptional ballplayer, the superstar, has a shot at cracking his line-up. I realized that he probably didn't consider me in the latter category inasmuch as I'd just been cut by a 3-11 team. I was crushed already.

We left the doctor's office and drove to the Dolphins training camp at Biscayne College. I was already frightened. To me Shula wasn't just another coach, he was a living legend. He and Vince Lombardi were frequently mentioned in the same breath by people who know about greatness. I'd sort of idolized the man, and here I was going to play for him. Maybe.

Shula had taken over a ragtag, inexperienced Dolphin team in 1970 and been in the play-offs every year since. I'd often wondered what might have happened had he gone to the Patriots instead. Would he have wound up in a strait jacket like the other coaches or would he have forged a winner? I was inclined to believe the latter.

I asked the equipment man about Shula. He spoke in terms of utter reverence, as if I'd asked the parish priest about the pope. I was scared to death already. Don Shula would be sitting behind a huge walnut desk going through papers and reviewing the day's activities. He would naturally be attired in handsome doubleknits and a green blazer, and he would probably have already forgotten about me.

✽

We drove through the campus gates and right over to the coaches' office. I was led in to be introduced to the coaches' coach, Don Shula. He was sprawled in a chair wearing a T-shirt and a jockstrap. I was amazed. I mean, who would have thought that Don Shula lounges around the office in his jock?

He welcomed me to the team and duly informed me that Fleming had signed his contract that afternoon. He said very simply that he'd keep me around and see what happened.

I could already see the handwriting on the wall. I had been brought down for insurance. The Dolphins were preparing for the College All-Star game and had Marvelous Marv not signed his new pact they'd have been in a bind for some experienced depth at tight end. Now Fleming's situation was all squared away. I hadn't put on a uniform yet and I was a lame duck already. But, at the very least, Shula had been honest with me.

I was surprised at the laxity of the Dolphin camp. I'd always assumed that a championship-caliber team like Miami must work its ass off in practice, but that didn't prove to be the case. The workouts were spirited, well organized, and efficient, but they weren't what you'd call back-breaking. Everyone was loose, and the coaches seemed to have an unusually good rapport with the players. Shula even led the team as we jogged around the field and went through calisthenics. And best of all, practices were short.

Another thing that appealed to me was the number of people who showed up to watch us practice. It wasn't uncommon to have 1000 fans watching a simple daily workout, and when we held our summer scrimmage — a controlled scrimmage, with the offense running the ball at the defensive unit — no less than 30,000 people showed up to watch. Thirty thousand spectators for an event that was essentially meaningless! Why, the Patriots had held a similar function each year and combined it with something called "picture day." Fans were allowed to roam at will with cameras among the players and snap away at will at any target that would hold still — which we were all, naturally, obliged to do. The largest turnout never exceeded 5000. Hell, in Miami they even had soft drink vendors in the stands at daily practice sessions.

*

Upon receiving my Dolphin playbook I recognized most of the running plays; they're essentially the same as the Patriots. The Dolphins pass plays, though, were wholly alien to anything I'd been accustomed to. I realized that it was well-nigh impossible to learn an entirely new system in just one week — and everyone else had been exposed to two weeks of practice when I arrived. At the same time, I had little cause to worry. I wasn't seeing enough playing time even in practice to have a chance to screw up by missing an assignment.

Mandich had come off the injured list, and he, Fleming, and Larry Seiple, the punter, worked out with the first three units. Shula had a rookie named Greg Boyd listed as the fourth tight end. I was running number five. I went through the motions and made the best of being in the Dolphin camp, but I was hardly brimming over with confidence.

The Miami players are, to a man, a super bunch of guys, and there's an impressive aura of mutual respect surrounding the entire team. That sort of thing happens when players have been through the wars together — and come out on top. Nick Buoniconti, in particular, was happy to see me. He inquired about the Patriots, and I told him of the changes that had been visited upon Foxboro, how where there once had been a coach there was now a king. Nick laughed and then said more seriously that getting away from that team had been the best thing that had ever happened to him. I felt the same way.

*

As if the week preceding the All-Star game wasn't hectic enough, Howard Cosell was in camp all week, shooting a special for ABC, and he was continually cutting up, enacting all the mischief Shula would let him get away with, perhaps a bit more. Cosell was in rare form. Besides interviewing several of the players and touring the locker room and dining area, he even worked out with some of the backs running plays. He had everyone in stitches. When he showed up for practice wearing a Dolphin uniform he looked like a pregnant praying mantis with his spaghetti-thin appendages and roly-poly midsection.

*

None of the Dolphins were particularly enthused by the prospect of playing the ambitious All-Stars. Manny Fernandez went on record, in fact, with the opinion that the All-Star game should be abolished. He hated it. Just another two weeks of work and a shot at getting hurt by some young hotshot out to make his mark.

On the other hand, I loved it. Unlike the other preseason games, the All-Star game provides the opportunity to collect a regular season game check. In other words, for an exhibition game in my case — as a veteran with more than five years' experience — the remuneration would be $335. For the college All-Star game I stood to collect $2000. With my career fast drawing to its conclusion and indefinite unemployment staring me in the face, that two grand was not at all insignificant.

As the days passed I became more anxious. I wasn't being asked to do anything in practice besides occasionally spell the tight end running the All-Star pass routes in dummy scrimmages. For the most part I just stood around. I was becoming obsessed with insecurity and the fear of being cut that week. Shula hadn't talked to me since I reported. It occurred to me that perhaps he'd forgotten I was there.

I tried to avoid him at all costs. If I saw him coming one way I'd go the other. I contemplated feigning injury but quickly dispelled that notion. It just wasn't my bag. I was the guy who had to look at myself in the mirror for the rest of my life. Hell, I thought, I'd played with torn ligaments in Denver one year and torn cartilage with the Patriots the past season. I wasn't going to let myself down.

Every night I checked the date off on my calendar. Monday passed, and then Tuesday. The $2000 was looking bigger every day, and there was still no word. I knew

Wednesday would be the day of reckoning. Since the game was to be played on Friday night, the team would leave on Thursday.

After practice I dressed quickly and bolted out of the dressing room in my haste to avoid Shula. As I opened the door I bumped right into him. I could feel the hair on my neck standing straight up; it was, after all, my first confrontation with the man since my arrival.

Suddenly he spoke to me. "Come into my office, Tom. I want to talk to you."

Damn! One day away from paydirt and I was caught like a rat in a trap. We both sat down in his office, and he looked me squarely in the eye: "We're going to take you to Chicago with us so you can collect the game check. Make your travel arrangements after Friday. Leave your playbook, and thanks for helping out."

What? I couldn't believe my ears. I could have kissed him. He hardly knew me or I him, but the man's class showed through his stern veneer. Here I was 1500 miles away from home and my NFL career had come to an end, yet Shula was showing his respect by taking me on the traveling squad to Chicago.

As I left the room the pieces began to fall into place in my mind. Shula was a winner, both on and off the field. It occurred to me that Joe Robbie had made the wisest move of his life when he had enticed Shula away from Baltimore. Not only was he a great football mind, he treated his players like men. I thanked my lucky stars that my last memories of the National Football League would be of Don Shula and not Chuck Fairbanks. I felt relieved.

*

The Chicago trip was, for me, just as if someone had given me an all-expenses-paid weekend at the All-Star game. I was even provided with a fifty-yard-line seat.

It was a nostalgic evening for me as I sat on the bench and watched the game. Just seven years before I'd begun my professional career on this same gridiron as a member of the All-Stars. Now it was coming to an end right here at Soldier Field.

I watched the All-Stars hustle through their warm-ups. Theirs was the same sort of enthusiasm I'd displayed when I'd played in this game; as I watched the collegians I could see myself. What a change, I thought, seven years has brought about in me. Everything I did now was methodical, pure business.

Nothing beats experience. The Dolphins simply acted out their roles, playing just hard enough to win. The All-Stars made mistakes, and we did not. It was a carbon copy of the game in which I'd played against the Green Bay Packers in 1967.

As I stood on the sideline watching the game I noticed a photographer snapping pictures. After striking up a conversation with him I managed to persuade him into taking a few shots of me while I was still a Dolphin. In a matter of minutes my career as a member of the World Champions would be over; hell, my name wasn't even listed on that night's game program.

He obliged and promised to send a few prints to me. I gave him my Boston address.

After the game we flew back to Miami. I decided to spend the weekend there. I figured I needed a vacation anyway. The trip back to Florida marked the first time in a month I'd been able to relax. I leaned back in my seat sipping Coors and listening to Doug Crusan and Manny Fernandez telling early Miami Dolphins stories, tales of the pre-Shula era when 35,000 was considered a good house in the Orange Bowl. They told stories about George Wilson and Bull Bramlett and Wahoo McDaniel, Rick Norton and Frank Emanuel. Stories that rivaled those I'd encountered with the Broncos and Patriots.

The difference was, of course, that the Dolphins veterans have seen the game from both sides of the fence. They'd gone from the ignominy of playing for chronic losers to Super Bowl champions.

I hadn't. I'd spent an entire career wallowing in mediocrity, but just being associated with Miami less than two weeks had provided me with an insight as to what the game is all about.

Winning.

*

I spent the weekend enjoying the hospitality of the Dolphins, swimming and sunning myself by the campus pool. On Sunday I made a reservation and split for Boston. My career as a Miami Dolphin had lasted ten days. As the plane glided upward I glanced through the cloud cover and bade farewell to Miami Beach. The dreams I'd engendered as I'd flown here less than two weeks ago had been painfully laid to rest. I knew that, at least for this year, I was done. My thoughts wandered back over the years I'd spent in the NFL, and I realized that even though most of them had been in the midst of chaos, turmoil, and despair, I was lucky. I probably wouldn't have traded places with anyone in the world. And now, the thought occurred to me as the plane approached for landing in Boston, for the first time in my life I was going out to meet my fate in the real world.

Epilogue

WHAT HAPPENS after that last hurrah? One day you're a household name, and the next day a trivia question. It was a great one for the bars:

Q. Who was Jim Whalen traded for?
A. Tom Beer.
Q. What's he doing now?
A. Collecting unemployment.

The words of Bucko Kilroy kept echoing through my mind. When asked by the daily papers why I was axed from the team, the Patriots chief talent scout chortled matter-of-factly: "Beer was a utility player." In other words, I wasn't big enough for the offensive line or fast enough for tight end. I guess I was only good enough until somebody else came to take my place.

After I was waived through the NFL I was faced with the task of going out and finding employment. Since the Canadian League was already in the middle of its season, there was no chance of a job there, so I busied myself doing some free-lance writing and a few radio talk shows. But mostly I wondered what the hell I was going to do with my life.

As the summer drew to a close I'd pretty much lost hope of catching on with an NFL team. I did, though, chance to have a drink with Danny Marr, one of the Patriots principal owners, who expressed his regrets that I wasn't in some way associated with the team. Danny even mentioned that Billy Sullivan had asked about me.

It was a ray of hope, albeit a slim one. And I *had* gone out of my way on a number of occasions to help the Patriots organization out. I doubt that anyone fulfilled more gratis speaking and public relations appearances than I did. I even took eleventh-hour calls when someone else couldn't make it at the last minute. I'm not trying to blow my own horn, I'm just trying to point out that I thought I deserved a better shake than I'd gotten from the Patriots after all I'd done for them. I'd played hurt. I'd suited up with torn cartilage in my knee and played. I couldn't jog without pain, but I'd played.

So I called the Patriots and asked them about some sort of job. They never got back to me. Admittedly, they were experiencing internal problems of their own. During the off season, Billy Sullivan would be voted out as Patriots president and replaced by Bob Marr. This move would lay to rest a lot of old conflicts.

During the season, I carefully followed the daily transactions to no avail. Tight ends are durable as hell. One of the only teams to bring in a tight end during the course of the year, ironically, was the Patriots. Bob Adams twisted an ankle and was deactivated for a month or so. My chances of being called back in this emergency situation were about as likely as there being a blizzard in Hawaii. The Patriots brought in a journeyman player named John Mosier, who had been with the Broncos, Colts, and Bills in the past four years.

I tried fraternizing with my old teammates but that natural closeness wasn't there. Professional athletes are a rare breed. Once your playing days have terminated, you're considered an outsider. Not "one of the boys" anymore. Believe me, adjusting to the straight life was no easy task. After playing football for the past twenty-two years, I was suddenly stripped of my identity. I was no longer Tom Beer, the jock. I was just Tom Beer. The thought scared me. My existence was suddenly an empty void.

Around the latter part of the '73 season intriguing little hints started appearing every so often in the papers. A new football league was being formed. The news was terse. Nothing more than a line or two. Gary Davidson, the innovative originator of the American Basketball Association and the World Hockey Association, was putting together a brand-new baby, the World Football League.

Curiosity overtook me. I called an old friend of mine, Will McDonough, to learn more about the situation. McDonough was very close to the WFL scene. He is a well-known sportswriter for the Boston *Globe,* so if anyone knew the guts of the WFL, it was McDonough.

He emphatically assured me Davidson's new league was no lark. "The WFL means business," he told me convincingly. "They have the bucks and are planning on twelve teams for the seventy-four season."

The Boston sportscasters and newspaper shills pooh-

poohed the speculation of a new pro football league. In Boston it is a mortal sin for the media people to show any positive interest in a new endeavor. Boston had the Patriots, what more could you ask for?

Subsequently, whenever something broke on the WFL, it was laughed off as a joke. Whoever would dare invade the hallowed soil and rattle the sacred ivory tower of the National Football League.

The sanctity of the National Football League was indeed violated by the WFL. In early December, the charter franchises in the new grid loop began being announced. NFL-dominated cities like Chicago, Detroit, and New York were granted franchises, as were the pro football-less hotbeds of Birmingham, Honolulu, and Jacksonville. Suddenly everything looked optimistic again.

Howard Baldwin, one of the owners of the New England Whalers, announced to the public shortly thereafter that a team would represent the city of Boston in the fledgling league. A couple of days later Baldwin called me and asked if I would be interested in joining his team in management. I reviewed my career in the NFL and reflected: would I be deserting the ship so to speak? After all, the NFL afforded me the opportunity of playing six complete seasons. I was classified as a vested veteran with full pension benefits at age fifty-five. Would I be a traitor in turning my back to the NFL and opting for the new league? How many people can say they played six years in the NFL?

As a matter of fact, a couple of NFL teams contacted me in December expressing interest in signing me to a contract for 1974. A couple more seasons in the NFL would enhance my existing pension even more.

Then I reflected on the way Fairbanks had treated me the past summer. The bitter taste of his putting me on waivers after one day of practice still rankled. You wouldn't treat a dog this way. My decision was easy. I jumped at the chance to be a part of the new challenge.

The rest is history. The league has come a long way in just eight short months. At a Super Bowl press conference last January, a reporter asked Pete Rozelle what he thought of the WFL. The NFL commissioner casually remarked that all he knew was what he read in the papers.

Now after the WFL has stripped the NFL of Larry Csonka, Jim Kiick, Paul Warfield, Ken Stabler, Ted Kwalick, and Calvin Hill, Rozelle must be a little concerned. The owners have learned all too late that professional football players have to look out for their best interests. They have to — the owners won't. The struggle between the owners and players is quite evident. There is a widening gap each year and Ed Garvey, the legal voice of the National Football League Players' Association, doesn't see the situation brightening.

In a show of power, the owners canceled the players' group insurance coverage as of March 31. The players came back with some term insurance of their own and threatened to strike if a new contract did not meet with their demands. The NFL situation is extremely gratifying to the WFL. As long as certain owners are around, players will be malcontent. Their dissatisfaction is the new league's salvation.

Of course the WFL will have no easy road to follow. The obstacles of formulating a successful endeavor like this will seem, at times, insurmountable. Even though it has won over the hearts of a number of genuine superstars, the league must win over the hearts of the populus. Tickets are bought by the fans.

While the concept of having a world league, with teams projected in Mexico City, Tokyo, and London, is exciting, nobody knows if American football will succeed in these foreign markets.

The overall concept of the WFL is definitely fan-oriented. The new rule innovations that have been bypassed by the NFL over the years suddenly have become our redemption. Kick-offs from the thirty-yard line, banning the fair catch on punts, and bringing a missed field goal back to the line of scrimmage are a few of the innovations that will put a lot of excitement into pro football. The excitement of an overtime period in case of a tie and the seven-point touchdown will enhance the game. The NFL, as it turned out, has had second thoughts concerning future rule changes. They decided to put some action in their staid game and boldly copied our new exciting rules. At the last owners' meeting the only item resolved of any consequence was giving Pete Rozelle a substantial raise. Now the NFL is deeply concerned. The WFL has even prodded the establishment into premature expansion.

In essence, the WFL has opened a lot of doors for players computerized out of football, players who have enough ability to play several more years, much to the chagrin of the pseudosophisticated minds of the NFL scouting elite. It will be fun watching these guys compete on the field once again. To many of them, football has been their life. They have been reincarnated, and their enthusiasm should be gratifying.

For me there is a whole new world ahead. Instead of

being forced into some position selling aluminum siding or toilet paper, I will remain in the sport that has been my entire life. My lifelong lover. My mistress.

I guess everything does work out for the best. My scars and bruises were worth it after all.

Tom Beer
Director of Player Personnel
New York Stars
World Football League